Exp⌐⌐⌐ ⌐g
BAKHTIN

Edited by Alastair Renfrew

with Contributions from

Roderick Watson
Alastair Renfrew
Graham Pechey
Donald Wesling
Pam Morris
and
Carol Adlam

Department Of Modern Languages,
University of Strathclyde, 1997

ISBN 0-9514164-3-X

Printed by the University of Strathclyde Print Unit

CONTENTS

The editor would like to thank everyone who helped organise and participated in the conference held at Strathclyde in March 1996, and who assisted in the preparation of this volume. Particular thanks go to Margaret Hamilton, Gordon Millan, Graham Roberts, Eamonn Rodgers, David Shepherd, Nijole White, and, of course, to all the contributors.

LIST OF ABBREVIATIONS

All references to works by Bakhtin are given using the following abbreviations and page numbers from, where possible, the English language edition. Publication details of the original Russian texts are given below.

AH   '**Author and Hero in Aesthetic Activity**', in *Art and Answerability: Early Philosophical Essays by M.M. Bakhtin*, ed. by Michael Holquist and Vadim Liapunov (University of Texas Press Slavic Series No. 9) (Austin: University of Texas Press, 1990), pp. 5–256.

'Avtor I geroi v esteticheskoi deiatel'nosti', in *Estetika slovesnogo tvorchestva*, ed. by S.G. Bocharov (Moscow: Isskustvo, 1979), pp. 7–180 [reprinted in *Raboty 1920–kh godov* (Kiev: Next, 1994), pp. 69–255].

DN   '**Discourse in the Novel**', in *The Dialogic Imagination: Four Essays by M.M. Bakhtin*, ed. by Michael Holquist; trans. by Caryl Emerson and Michael Holquist (University of Texas Press Slavic Series No. 1) (Austin: University of Texas, 1981), pp. 259–422.

'Slovo v romane', in *Voprosy literatury i estetiki: Issledovaniia raznykh let*, ed. by S. Leibovich (Moscow: Khudozhestvennaia literatura, 1975), pp. 72–233.

EN   '**Epic and Novel**', in *The Dialogic Imagination: Four Essays by M.M. Bakhtin*, ed. by Michael Holquist; trans. by Caryl Emerson and Michael Holquist (University of Texas Press Slavic Series No. 1) (Austin: University of Texas, 1981), pp. 3–41.

'Epos i roman: o metodologii issledovaniia romana', in *Voprosy literatury i estetiki: Issledovaniia raznykh let*, ed. by S. Leibovich (Moscow: Khudozhestvennaia literatura, 1975), pp. 447–83.

MHS 'Toward a Methodology for the Human Sciences', in *Speech Genres and Other Late Essays*, trans. by Vern W. McGee; ed. by Caryl Emerson and Michael Holquist (University of Texas Press Slavic Series No. 8) (Austin: University of Texas Press, 1986), pp. 159–77.

'K metodologii gumanitarnykh nauk', in *Estetika slovesnogo tvorchestva*, ed. by S.G. Bocharov (Moscow: Isskustvo, 1979), 361–73.

N70 'Notes Made in 1970–71', in *Speech Genres and Other Late Essays*, trans. by Vern W. McGee; ed. by Caryl Emerson and Michael Holquist (University of Texas Press Slavic Series No. 8) (Austin: University of Texas Press, 1986), pp. 159–77.

'Iz zapisei 1970–1971 godov', in *Estetika slovesnogo tvorchestva*, ed. by S.G. Bocharov (Moscow: Isskustvo, 1979), pp. 336–60.

PDP *Problems of Dostoevsky's Poetics*, ed. and trans. by Caryl Emerson (Minneapolis and London: University of Minnesota Press, 1984).

Problemy poetiki Dostoevskogo (Moscow: Sovetskii pisatel', 1963) [reprinted in *Problemy tvorchestva/poetiki Dostoevskogo* (Kiev: Next, 1994), pp. 205–492].

PSG 'The Problem of Speech Genres', in *Speech Genres and Other Late Essays*, trans. by Vern W. McGee; ed. by Caryl Emerson and Michael Holquist (University of Texas Press Slavic Series No. 8) (Austin: University of Texas Press, 1986), pp. 60–102.

'Problema rechevykh zhanrov', in *Estetika slovesnogo tvorchestva*, ed. by S.G. Bocharov (Moscow: Isskustvo, 1979), pp. 237–80 [reprinted in *Sobranie sochinenii,* vol. 5 (Moscow: Russkii slovar', 1996), pp. 159–206].

PT 'The Problem of the Text in Linguistics, Philology, and the Human Sciences: An Experiment in Philosophical Analysis', in *Speech Genres and Other Late Essays*, trans. by Vern W. McGee; ed. by Caryl Emerson and Michael Holquist (University of Texas Press Slavic Series No. 8) (Austin: University of Texas Press, 1986), pp. 103–31.

'Problema teksta v lingvistike, filologii I drugikh gumanitarnykh naukakh. Opyt filosofskogo analiza', in *Estetika slovesnogo tvorchestva*, ed. by S.G. Bocharov (Moscow: Isskustvo, 1979), pp. 281–307 [reprinted as 'Problema teksta', in *Sobranie sochinenii,* vol. 5 (Moscow: Russkii slovar', 1996), pp. 306–26].

RQ '**Response to a Question from the Staff of** *Novyi mir*', in *Speech Genres and Other Late Essays*, trans. by Vern W. McGee; ed. by Caryl Emerson and Michael Holquist (University of Texas Press Slavic Series No. 8) (Austin: University of Texas Press, 1986), pp. 1–9.

'Otvet na vopros redaktsii *Novogo mira*', in *Estetika slovesnogo tvorchestva*, ed. by S.G. Bocharov (Moscow: Isskustvo, 1979), pp. 328–35.

RW *Rabelais and His World*, trans. by Hélène Iswolsky (Bloomington: Indiana, 1984).

Tvorchestva Fransua Rable i narodnaia kul'tura srednevekov'ia i Renessansa (Moscow: Khudozhestvennaia literatura, 1965) [reprinted 1990].

TPA *Toward a Philosophy of the Act*, trans. by Vadim Liapunov; ed. by Vadim Liapunov and Michael Holquist (University of Texas Press Slavic Series No. 10) (Austin: University of Texas Press, 1993).

'K filosofii postupka', in *Filosofiia i sotsiologiia nauki i tekhniki: Ezhegodnik 1984–1985* (Moscow: Nauka, 1986), 80-160 [reprinted in *Raboty 1920–kh godov* (Kiev: Next, 1994), pp. 9–68].

Introduction: Bakhtin, Victim of Whose Circumstance?

Alastair Renfrew

> [Bakhtin] lived a long and difficult life, not only in the purely bio-
> graphical sense, but also in the academic sense. A long and, it
> would appear, no less difficult fate awaits him in the memory of
> culture.[1]

Our initial response to any writer or critic from the Soviet period who
did not enjoy at least some degree of state sponsorship is to approach
his or her work as the work, more or less, of a *victim* of political or
ideological circumstance. Such a response is in Bakhtin's case no less
justified for its acquiescence in stereotype, particularly if we restrict
ourselves to consideration of the lived experience of Bakhtin as an individual. This might explain the continued interest among Russian
scholars in Bakhtin's biography, a subject likely to provoke only marginal interest among his Western interpreters. The Western observer of
the Soviet period is, however, liable to be tempted by the following
formula for the relation of the biography to the work itself: 'were it not
for Soviet power, Bakhtin's dialogism would never have existed'.[2]
Yet such formulae are more likely to be productive of an analysis
which is only peripherally concerned with Bakhtin; the paradox facing
Bakhtin studies in the West is that it is those who are exclusively or at
least primarily concerned with the substance of what Bakhtin wrote
who are in danger of inflicting upon him a new 'victimhood', who are
in the process of making him a victim, specifically, *of our own circumstances*. The constant flow of material devoted to the interpretation, extension and application of Bakhtin's ideas has taken little account of the fundamental difficulties which have attended their passage
into Western literary and cultural theory.[3] This has led not only to the
devaluation of particular analyses of Bakhtin as new primary sources
are published or promised, but also, in a gargantuan academic para-

---

[1] L. A. Gogotishvili, 'Varianty i invarianty M. M. Bakhtina', *Voprosii filosofii*, 1 (1992), 115–
134 (p. 115).
[2] Mikhail Sokolov attributes this to a conversation with A. Gulyga in 'Bakhtin and Warburg:
Elective Affinities in Dialogical Cultural Studies', in Adlam, Falconer, Makhlin and Renfrew
(eds.), *Face to Face: Bakhtin in Russia and the West* (Sheffield: Sheffield Academic Press, 1997
[forthcoming]).
[3] The Bakhtin Bibliographical Database at the Bakhtin Centre, Sheffield University details 68
monographs in the English language alone; the MLA Bibliography will return a staggering *thousand* Bakhtin-related articles.

phrase of conspicuous consumption, to a point where Bakhtin can begin to appear to have been exhausted even before he has been properly assimilated. The following remarks are offered, then, not as any kind of resolution of this problem, but rather in a wholly questioning spirit, save perhaps for the conviction that the issue of the *use* we have for Bakhtin must be resolved prior to any of the substantive issues raised in his work.

The first problem requiring attention concerns the way in which the fate of Bakhtin the individual relates not somehow to the content of the work (a problem I am neither inclined nor qualified to address), but relates rather to what I'm also going to term the 'fate' of the work, i.e., the material circumstances of its publication and translation. The fact that Bakhtin's output was not published in anything like the order in which it was written, but was substantially reconstructed from manuscripts in greater or lesser degrees of 'completion', with or without the assistance of Bakhtin himself, will undoubtedly trouble some more than others. But this immediate chronological disordering constitutes an inherent level of instability, to which we must add the following: the process of Bakhtin's translation into English has followed neither the order of production nor the order of publication; further, even if we put aside the question of the 'possibility' of translation, dearly beloved of Russians and Russianists alike, it must at least be noted that the 'accuracy' of available English translations varies considerably (the *Rabelais* book and *Speech Genres and Other Late Essays* being notably less reliable). Finally, and most crucially, any project of 'complete translation', if not quite premature, would at least be temporarily disabled, because the process of publication or 'reconstruction' of Bakhtin in Russian is itself incomplete, and continues at a pace and in a degree of secrecy which, until very recently, we might have been forgiven for characterizing as 'Soviet'. It must be hoped that the publication of the 'first' volume of the *Complete Works* in Moscow late last year signals the beginning of the end of the process of making the entire body of work available in Russian and, subsequently, in English.[4] It is interesting to note that this release has had a complex effect on expectations as to what remains to be published for the first time: it confirms, on the one hand, that 'The Problem of Speech Genres' was not a limited or isolated essay upon the subject; but, on the other, it

---

[4] The volume in question is actually No. 5 in a series of 7; M.M. Bakhtin, *Sobranie sochinenii*, vol. 5 (Moscow: Russkii slovar', 1996).

would also appear to deny once and for all the existence of a book entitled *Genres of Speech* [*Zhanry rechi*], said in the notes to *Estetika slovesnogo tvorchestva* to have been planned by Bakhtin 'in the 1950s–1970s'.[5] It would be possible to say that the prospect of any-thing relatively 'major' emerging from Bakhtin's personal archive re-mains faint, but such a statement would absolutely require qualifica-tion. The fragment subsequently entitled *Toward a Philosophy of the Act* (1920–23) appeared in Russian as recently as 1986, and in English translation in 1993, and had the effect of provoking the re-evaluation of much later and more substantial texts, effectively re-invigorating not only the central debate on Bakhtin's principal object of investigation in terms of 'discipline', but also the question of the extent to which he is a 'philosopher' of the personal or of the collective. But we may be forgiven for asking how often will we be required to 'rethink Bak-htin'?[6] What would now constitute 'major' in the context of such an exhaustively deployed body of work? A lost book on the *Bildungsro-man*, perhaps; or the detailed outline of such a book;[7] further primary evidence of the influence on Bakhtin of German and Russian neo-Kantianism? No-one, it seems, outside of Sergei Bocharov, executor of the archive and editor (along with L.A. Gogotishvili) of the *Complete Works*, can be sure as to what exactly remains to be published even in Russian.[8] The particular blend of certainty and doubt which surrounds this issue has produced a situation where it is acceptable to *cite* the supposed 'contents' of an archive not yet in the public domain *in any language*: for example, a recent article, the citation of which I am sure the author will forgive, supports the hypothesis that Bakhtin was famil-iar with the works of Lukács with quotation of a conversation with Bo-

[5] Tzvetan Todorov refers to this 'work' in his *Mikhail Bakhtin: The Dialogical Principle* (Manchester: Manchester University Press, 1984), p. 5, as *The Genres of Discourse*. Todorov usefully summarises 'books begun or outlined but never finished', but goes on to confess that 'there is no guarantee' that even the quite staggering array of material to which he refers 'is ex-haustive' (pp. 5–6).
[6] Gary Saul Morson and Caryl Emerson's *Rethinking Bakhtin: Extensions and Challenges* (Evanston, Illinois: Northwestern Univ. Press, 1989) was substantially occasioned by the Russian publication of TPA.
[7] Brian Poole, 'Mikhail Bakhtin i teoriia romana vospitaniia' [Mikhail Bakhtin and the Theory of the *Bildungsroman*], in *M.M. Bakhtin i perspektivy gumanitarnykh nauk* [Mikhail Bakhtin and Prospects for the Human Sciences] (Vitebsk, 1994), pp. 62–71 (p. 63).
[8] It was originally intended that this volume would contain a bibliography of works published in Russian since 1986 which have not yet been translated into English; in the light of the publica-tion of volume 5 of the *Complete Works*, however, such a bibliography could not hope to be 'complete', even on its own specifically limited terms.

charov and the footnote: 'Details and documentary evidence will be
withheld for the present'.[9]

This brief description of the material circumstances in which we find
Bakhtin, and the caution they implicitly prescribe for our responses to
him, are assuredly not enough, however, to render us in any sense *cul-
pable* in our interpretations and applications. We are all, on the most
pragmatic level, constrained to work with whatever happens to be ac-
cessible. Equally, it is possible to argue that notions of a 'complete' or
'transparent' canon are in any case inherently spurious, and likely to
hinder rather than facilitate understanding; I should stress that I am not
advocating the pursuit of some kind of 'totalizing narrative' in Bakhtin.
But what animates this background, transforming a degree of uncertainty into a potentially immobilising debility, where the issue becomes
the very viability of any Western Bakhtinian project, are the circumstances *in which Bakhtin finds us.*

It is only fair in this connection to begin by examining those circumstances from the correlating 'other' point of view, that is, from a specifically Russian perspective. It is of only marginal relevance, perhaps,
that there is a fairly consistent presumption among Russian Bakhtinians
that non-Russian speakers are inevitably disadvantaged, although to
ignore this completely would be to enhance rather than diminish that
relevance. Nor should the question of our 'cultural otherness' detain
us: perceptions of 'cultural otherness' are inevitably, inherently and
perfectly two-sided, and reliance on notions of the deficient perspective of anyone other than 'ourselves' is perfectly self-reflexive, and
self-defeating. In any case, at least one version of Bakhtin's theory of
social and/or inter-subjective relations explicitly privileges the element
of exteriority or outsideness, posits the necessity of 'the Other' in the
finalization of a given subject.

The charge which most demands our attention, however, is simply
that Western interpreters of Bakhtin have a far greater *need* of him
than Bakhtin, and by extension his Russian followers, have of Western
responses and extensions. The most perceptive of Russian Bakhtinians
seem to have realised that literary and cultural studies in Britain and
North America, while not quite 'in crisis', have certainly ceased to be
quite as 'focused', in one way or another, as they have been since the
'advent of theory'. There is an appreciation of the fact that an array of
post-Saussurean attempts to locate language and writing (and power,

---

[9] Galin Tihanov, 'Bakhtin, Lukács and Literary Genre', in *Slovo*, 8.2 (1995), 44–52 (p. 45).

and the social, and the subconscious...) have perhaps failed to deliver the 'scientific' discipline implicitly or even explicitly promised, or have failed even to chart a course for their own further development. Equally, there is an appreciation that diverse tendencies in literary and cultural studies, having imbibed (or externalised) a theoretical animus, might be reluctant or unable to return to a retrenched 'humanist' position; to return to what is, not perhaps too ironically, Bakhtin's own point of embarkation in the early and posthumously published work to which I have already referred, *Toward a Philosophy of the Act*. It is Bakhtin's characteristic ability to retain a foot in both of these 'camps', to look in two directions simultaneously, that makes him so attractive to contemporary literary and cultural studies—and where, we might ask, is the problem in that? The problem as defined by Vitalii Makhlin, one of the most persuasive of current Russian Bakhtinians, is that Western interpreters across a broad range of subject areas simply appropriate Bakhtin for their own purposes and purely in their own terms: in a series of selective approaches to an already unstable 'canon' each succeeds only in making Bakhtin a *double of his or her own self*. Whilst accepting the definitive power of this challenge (in the proper sense of that word) to Western responses to Bakhtin, it is however necessary once again, as in relation to the question of 'cultural otherness', to emphasise that there can be no possibility of total immunity to this syndrome; there is no absolutely and implicitly 'privileged' interpreter, protected by greater knowledge of self and other.

Returning then to our own, Western perspective, might not the suspicion linger that those hundreds of articles and dozens of books, taken as a species rather than in all their specific diversity, represent nothing other than the hasty and indiscriminate application of a resource whose appeal has been enhanced largely by the exhaustion of other resources? The difficulty here is not that Bakhtin has appeared 'providential' in respect of the full range of humanistic disciplines from anthropology to political science, or that his influence has so thoroughly penetrated disciplines such as literary studies, through any subject area within that discipline, however defined; the difficulty is rather what this breadth of appeal brings with it, and that is the implication that any and every such subject area or broader discipline (though this applies particularly in literary and/or cultural studies) somehow *must* be explored through the medium of Bakhtin, lest it begin to appear comparatively impoverished 'without him'. If the contention that certain issues are by definition 'inappropriate' or alien to Bakhtin (feminisms, marxisms; cinema/theatre), whether because he neglects to discuss them or appears to reject them in his own work, is assuredly absurd, so then, from the diametrically opposite point of view, are shallow applications or extensions detrimental to the rejection of that initial contention.

The verb 'to exploit' carries within it at least two distinct meanings: the first is broadly pejorative, where 'exploitation' tends towards synonymy with 'abuse' and regard for the object of 'exploitation' is wholly dissolved in its purpose or intent; the second is more neutral, or 'technical', the very act of 'exploiting' implying the value of the resource to be exploited, its aptness or *necessity* to the purpose for which it is intended. The articles in this collection, which purposely range across a number of subjects, are offered then as *essays* under the sign of the latter shade of meaning, yet which retain an awareness of the perils of the former. Roderick Watson's essay is broadly affirmative of Bakhtin's potential for the invigoration of critical approaches to Scottish writing, seeing the combination of sensitivity to the linguistic entropy and (Rabelaisian) extremity which have been central to the Scottish tradition as virtually irresistible. My own contribution, while affirming the relevance of certain Bakhtinian models for a 'native' theory of literature, nevertheless cautions against the straightforward identification of dialect or 'non-standard' Englishes with Bakhtin's notion of a heteroglot, dialogized literature. These essays were, incidentally, completed 'in the knowledge' of one another, and my own at least is considerably improved for that exposure.

Graham Pechey shifts the focus away from the localised concerns of Scottish writing and culture and onto the recent cultural history of South Africa as a more generalised representative of the postcolonial condition. Pechey reviews his own past work on the subject, invoking Bakhtin as a powerful means of formulating new and productive models of authority and tradition in the constantly evolving field of relations between the 'centre' and the 'margins', always with the proviso that 'we are each of us a margin and each of us a centre'.

Donald Wesling treats a subject which has floated in and out of Bakhtin studies, never quite resolved, never quite decisively ignored, namely Bakhtin's apparent distaste for the poetic genres. Wesling offers poetic *rhythm* as the ground upon which Bakhtin's 'wrong turn' might be corrected, developing his argument through a reading of Marina Tsvetaeva's 'Wires' which is both illustrative of his hypothesis and, intriguingly, perfectly self-sufficient.

Broadly feminist readings of Bakhtin have remained among the most controversial and, perhaps consequentially, the most stimulating of Western extensions of his work, often provoking the scorn of Russian interpreters and conservative westerners alike. Pam Morris's essay is an avowed attempt to position Bakhtin's earliest substantial works, *Toward a Philosophy of the Act* and 'Author and Hero in Aesthetic Activity', in relation to the work of Julia Kristeva and Gayatri Spivak on the location of a specifically feminine subject in the production of literary texts. Morris devotes a substantial portion of the essay to comparative and separate analyses of the work of Angela Carter and Mahasweta Devi.

Finally, Carol Adlam, in an essay which gives a great deal of valuable bibliographical information without ever becoming simply a 'bibliographical essay', explicitly addresses the ideological and cultural issues which threaten to render any dialogue between Russian and Western Bakhtinians mutually unintelligible, chief among which are respective responses to the illusions of 'centrality' and 'authority'.

It will be immediately clear that although certain of the above subjects are more familiar than others in a Bakhtinian context (the majority in fact taking at least their initial motivation from the 'literary' domain), none, in its specifics, can be said to have occupied anything like a central position in Bakhtin studies, either in Russia or in the West. This is perhaps because the respective concerns of each contributor are almost by definition resistant to any illusion of centrality. It will also become clear as the reader progresses through the collection that the extent to which each individual essay is centred on these subjects, as opposed to being 'centred' on Bakhtin, varies greatly; Bakhtin is variously a sounding-board for perceptions on a given theme, an 'immovable object' against which to struggle in the development of another, and indeed the primary animus of particular essays. Such variety, both in theme and in the location of Bakhtin in relation to it, gives rise to the temptation to impose some kind of order or unified direction on the whole; the ubiquitous Bakhtinian *caveat* with regard to the finalization of (various) others makes this temptation relatively easy to resist, however, and the reader may make his or her own choices in this respect. As to the task of 'seeing oneself', of assessing the initiating intent of this collection, that too, although on the basis of a potentially contradictory *caveat*, is best left to the reader.

Speaking in Tongues:
Reflections after Bakhtin on the Scots Literary Tradition and Contemporary Writing

Roderick Watson

Let us begin with two quotations—speaking in tongues, indeed:

> There are, it may be, so many kinds of voices in the world, and none of them is without signification.
> Therefore if I know not the meaning of the voice, I shall be unto him that speaketh a barbarian, and he that speaketh shall be a barbarian unto me.

This comes from first Corinthians 14: 10,11, but in this context it should also call up echoes of Douglas Dunn's concept of the Scottish poet (or a northern English poet such as, say, Tony Harrison) as another kind of 'barbarian'. The second quotation comes from the speech that James Kelman made when he won the Booker prize in 1994, dealing with another account of that which is beyond the pale, below the salt, of what is 'not us':

> A couple of weeks ago a feature writer for a Quality newspaper suggested that the use of the term 'culture' was inappropriate in relation to my work, that the characters peopling my pages were 'pre-culture'—or was it 'primeval'? I can't quite recall. This was explicit, generally it isn't. But—as Tom Leonard pointed out more than 20 years ago—the gist of the argument amounts to the following, that vernaculars, patois, slangs, dialects, gutter-languages etc. etc. might well have a place in the realms of comedy (and the frequent references to Connolly or *Rab C. Nesbitt* substantiate this) but they are inferior linguistic forms and have no place in literature. And *a priori* any writer who engages in the use of such so-called language is not really engaged in literature at all.[1]

This paper concerns itself with the points at which poetics and politics are engaging with each other in current Scottish writing. It will examine some of the ways in which Bakhtinian concepts can be used to describe and to analyse aspects of Scottish culture, and it will end by considering what can be described as a new Rabelaisian strain in contemporary Scottish fiction, and the questions raised by this writing

---

[1] Published in 'Spectrum', *Scotland on Sunday*, 16 October, 1994.

about what 'carnivalia' (beyond the comforts of academe) might actually entail in today's civil and secular society. The struggle between discourses has always been political, and the Bakhtinian model adopted here is one which would interpret such struggle as a dynamic and constantly changing interplay between centrifugal and centripetal forces, going on to show how that conflict will simultaneously demonstrate and create various discursive forms, social effects and different tendencies in representation.

Scottish culture has been a particularly fruitful and appropriate field for such study, because polyglossia, along with linguistic, social, political and national tensions concerning the influence of English culture and rule from Westminster, have been significantly present in our literature since at least the Union of 1707:

> The 'vernacularisation' of Scots in the eighteenth century revival has sometimes been seen as a reductive process—a slide into genre literature—and certainly poems such as 'Bonny Heck' do little to dispel such an impression. On the other hand, the growing potency of the 'Christis Kirk' tradition can be seen as an upsurge of the old carnival spirit, comic and subversive, a 'reductive idiom' full of oral energy and folk irreverence in the face of a political and linguistic agenda which was increasingly centralising and monological in its aspirations. (The Union of 1707, after all, marked the beginning of 'Great Britain' and the first steps towards the formal concept of a British empire). On the literary front, the prevailingly neoclassical values of [Enlightenment Scotland] and 'good' writing in England emphasised lucidity, balance, and universal applicability, not at all the same thing as a delight in energy and contradiction, or in mixing the resolutely local with high flown idealism or metaphysical aspiration. (This is not to say that such energy cannot be found in English literature—in Swift, for example—but it was not adopted, as it plainly was in Scotland, as a national 'voice').[2]

That 'voice' as (paradoxically) realised in a modified and printed literary form, turned out to be highly heterodox and unstable in the most creative way. In the eighteenth century, for example, the poetry of

[2] Roderick Watson, 'Dialectics of "Voice" and "Place": Literature in Scots and English from 1700', in Paul H. Scott (ed.), *Scotland. A Concise Cultural History* (Edinburgh: Mainstream, 1993), pp. 99–125 (p. 103). See also the past and present critical traces of these issues in Edwin Muir, *Scott and Scotland: The Predicament of the Scottish Writer* (London. Routledge, 1936); David Daiches, *The Paradox of Scottish Culture: The Eighteenth Century Experience* (London: Oxford University Press, 1964); Kenneth Simpson, *The Protean Scot: The Crisis of Identity in Eighteenth Century Scottish Literature* (Aberdeen: Aberdeen University Press, 1988); Robert Crawford, *Devolving English Literature* (Oxford: Clarendon Press, 1992).

Ramsay, Fergusson and Burns was inscribed and interpenetrated by different dialects of Scots, as well as by English words, in a variety of different registers and literary genres. And by the time we come to the modern literary revival of 'Lallans' or what Douglas Young called 'Plastic Scots', long poem sequences such as *A Drunk Man Looks at the Thistle* (1926), or Sydney Goodsir Smith's *Under the Eildon Tree* (1948), can be shown to be polyphonous and heteroglossial to an outstanding degree.

Goodsir Smith's work lends itself well to a brief demonstration of the heteroglossic and subversive power of such Scottish writing in a modernist context, and it may even suggest that such fluidity is directly born out of the difficult relationships that must inevitably exist between a despised native tongue and the political, cultural and economic hegemony of a larger nation and a relatively standardized literary discourse. In *Under the Eildon Tree* it is Elegy V, 'Slugabed', which introduces the persona of the poet himself, lying in bed in the middle of the day, like Oblomov:

> Here I ligg, Sydney Slugabed Godless Smith,
> The Smith, the Faber, *Poyetas* and Makar,
> And Oblomov has nocht to learn me,
> Auld Oblomov has nocht on me
> Liggan my lane in bed at nune
> Gantan at gray December haar,   mist
> A cauld, scummie, hauf-drunk cup o' tea
>   At my bed-side,
>   Luntan Virginia fags
> –The new world thus I haud in fief
> And levie kyndlie tribute. Black men slave
> Aneth a distant sun to mak for me
> Cheroots at hauf-a-croon the box.
> Wi ase on the sheets, ase on the cod,   pillow
> And crumbs of toast under my bum,
> Scrievan the last great coronach   Gaelic lament
> O' the westren flickeran bourgeois world.
>   *Eheu fugaces!*
>   *Lacrimae rerum!*
> *Nil nisi et caetera ex cathedra*
>   *Requiescat* up your jumper.[3]

---

[3] 'Elegy V' from 'Under the Eildon Tree', in Sydney Goodsir Smith, *Collected Poems 1941–1975* (London: John Calder, 1975), p. 154.

This is good irreverent fun, but the passage is a bit more disruptive than it may seem at first. The reference to Oblomov alerts us to the text's intellectual pretensions, while the colloquial force of its utterance might seem to shake them. Thus the lines simultaneously enjoy and mock the status of the self-consciously 'Bohemian' writer, and maybe even the act of writing altogether. Certainly it goes on to make a critique of unearned authorial status by questioning the unexamined privileges by which he is free to write. It might even suggest that the freedom to write his last lament for the western world is actually subsidised by the world of affairs and the bourgeois empire he affects to despise: 'Black men slave/Aneth a distant sun to mak for me/Cheroots at hauf-a-croon the box.'

The collage of Latin tags at the end lays claim to classical authority, but it also despises and deconstructs that authority. Even so, the fragments do speak a kind of truth. 'Alas the years go flying by'; 'the tears of things', and 'speak nothing but good of the dead', all relate to passing time, age, and fading powers. On the other hand, although Popes and authors may speak *ex cathedra*, this author cannot complete any of these Latin phrases, and the only thing that comes from his throne is '*Nothing unless etc*' and '*Requiescat*', (the first word of an epitaph), followed by the colloquial vulgarity 'up your jumper'.

The literary power of this voice is undeniable. Smith's long poem sequence uses ancient and modern usages, switching from 'high' to 'low' and back again with bewildering speed. His verse is dense with quotations (or tags) from French, Greek, Latin, Italian, German, Russian and Scots and English texts, plus parodic versions of RP English and American diction. These multiple ironies and registers entertain and fascinate us every bit as much as the self-reflexive discourses of the underground man or Makar Devushkin.[4] But will 'Slugabed Smith' inherit the earth any more than they will? (His identification with ineffectual Oblomov is a telling one.) The underground man's argument with himself is as much an index of his isolation as it is a measure of his dialogical irreverence, and we may well come to feel that Smith's wild polyphony is nothing less, in the end, than another such discourse of powerlessness?

---

[4] Bakhtin analyses such discourse and reconstructs Devushkin's self utterance as a version of dialogue in *Problems of Dostoevsky's Poetics*, ed. and trans. by Caryl Emerson (Manchester: Manchester University Press, 1984), pp. 204–37.

In responding to the marvellous parody, fluidity, energy and instability of such 'speaking in tongues', we may have to ask ourselves whether it might also reflect a desperate insecurity and a final sense of disconnection? Are these no more than the signals of the subaltern (to borrow a term from postcolonial theory) forever condemned to sit on the sidelines, imitating or pulling faces at those forces which really command us?[5] Perhaps this is the only voice that is left to us when we are denied access to any discourse other than that of carnivalia? And the celebration of 'irreverent' freedom may be no more than a rattling of chains.

But representation is subtle, and the mere presence of such polyphony may be more powerful and destabilising than at first it seems. However small, it is still a hugely positive step for such voices to be able to enter the institutional sphere—even just to be *heard* in the corridors of the academy. (Nevertheless, at this point we must also register the possibility—a familiar doubt—that the licence of carnivalia merely permits what it sets out to guy. The word 'licence', after all, has a deadly double meaning.)

Having said that, there's still no doubt that the Bakhtinian concepts of dialogical processes, Rabelaisian excess and heteroglossia have become very valuable models for defining and discussing the Scottish literary and cultural tradition *vis-à-vis* its English neighbour; and Bakhtin's terms have entered the current critical discourse in what seem to me an entirely positive way, by which questions of Scottish identity are rephrased as questions of identities, and 'Scotland' redefined as Scotlands. (Note, however, that these properties are never supposed to be exclusive to Scotland, but only—perhaps for the historical reasons cited above—peculiarly apposite.)

Here is Robert Crawford's passionate defence of Scottish linguistic fluidity in the last chapter of his book on 'Self and Territory in Twentieth-Century Poetry'. Crawford starts by evoking the concept of hybridity, which is now, perhaps, more familiar in terms of postcolonial theory, although he does not name it as such:

---

[5] See, for example, Gayatri Spivak, 'Can the Subaltern Speak?', in *Marxism and the Interpretation of Culture*, ed. by Cary Nelson and Lawrence Grossberg (London: Macmillan, 1988), pp. 271–313; and Homi Bhabha, 'Of Mimicry and Man: the Ambivalence of Colonial Discourse', in *Modern Literary Theory*, ed. by Philip Rice and Patricia Waugh, 2nd edition (London: Edward Arnold, 1993), pp. 234–41.

> We know that impurity of language matters as much as purity; be-
> cause in impurity lies richness, imagination and the seeds of new
> growth. Homogeneity—who needs it? Dictators, racists, Scots
> Style-sheeters, prescriptivists who want us all the same. Where is
> the homogeneity in MacDiarmid's synthetic Scots, or Burns's syn-
> thetic Scots for that matter? Homogeneity is the enemy of Scottish
> culture, which is and has been for centuries fundamentally, linguisti-
> cally pluralist.[6]

But such pluralism cannot and must not simply be a recipe for liberal
relativism and an unproblematic celebration of difference for difference's sake. Nor can it be enough to cite heterogeneity as an uncom-
plicated ideal, for some of the clashes and subversions implicit in heteroglossial and dialogical discourse surely do reveal mutually contradictory positions and real schisms. Differences which involve real
challenges for literary authority (and hence social, political and moral
authority) must command serious critical and ethical examination.

Tom Leonard and James Kelman, among more recent Scottish writers, have never doubted the vital connection between poetics and politics, as the following comments from Kelman make clear:

> The stories I wanted to write would derive from my own back-
> ground, my own socio-cultural experience. I wanted to write as one
> of my own people, I wanted to write and remain a member of my
> own community.[7]

But when he looked at how the Scots working class was represented in
literature (or indeed 'anybody from any regional part of Britain'), he
could find only stereotypes, linguistically separated from their authors,
and 'characterised' by their accents. Kelman's account of this situation
has no truck with the comforts of liberal pluralism:

> [...] unlike the nice stalwart upperclass English hero (occasionally
> Scottish but with no linguistic variation) whose words on the page
> were always absolutely splendidly proper and pure and pristinely
> accurate, whether in dialogue or without. And what grammar!

---

[6] Robert Crawford, *Identifying Poets: Self and Territory in Twentieth-Century Poetry*
(Edinburgh: Edinburgh University Press, 1993), p. 162. If I had to cite contemporary examples
of the creative rewards of such heterogeneity, I would point to the gloriously hybrid and yet intensely local cultures evoked by John Byrne's writing, first with rock and roll in *Tutti Frutti*, and
then with country music in the wild west of Scotland in *Your Cheatin' Heart*.
[7] James Kelman, from *Some Recent Attacks: Essays Cultural and Political* (Stirling: A.K. Press,
1992), p. 81.

Colons and semi-colons! Straight out of their mouths! An incredi-
ble mastery of language. Most interestingly of all, for myself as a
writer, the narrative belonged to them and them alone. They owned
it. The place where thought and spiritual life exists. (Kelman, 82)

Kelman's project ever since has been to close the gap between diegetic
and mimetic discourse, to find a way of inscribing thought and spiritual
life in what many commentators still see as the severely limited linguistic field of urban demotic utterance, or which they still interpret as
simply transcribed speech or an entirely oral medium somehow
'written down'. Even so, Kelman's diegetic authorial presence has not
been relinquished (in the last analysis, how could it be?) and his texts
(especially his early texts) can be shown to enact a high degree of literary awareness in an intertextual heteroglossia which operates in vivid
and often multiply subversive ways.[8] It must be admitted, however,
that such heteroglossia has been less evident in Kelman's most recent
work, and in the paper which immediately follows this one Alastair
Renfrew proposes that Kelman's agenda has actually been to strive
against heteroglossia, towards the 'pure single voice' of extended dialect narrative: the very 'antithesis of diversity of speech'.[9] I would
agree that Kelman has indeed reduced linguistic diversity in, for example, *How late it was, how late* (1994) where the narrative register
and the mimetic register of the protagonist's speech or inner life do
seem to merge. At the same time, it is important to recognise that the
result is not monologue, for a separate narrative position does remain.
Nor is it anything like stream of consciousness, since Kelman resolutely refuses to claim any hint of omniscient privilege over his characters' inner workings.

Nevertheless, however 'monological' the diegetic voice may become, this question cannot be resolved by a purely technical and textual analysis, for in the interrelationship between poetics and politics
matters of narrative and linguistic authority go beyond the page itself,
and must be related to questions of genre in the first instance, and then
to the further reaches of institutional and ideological hegemony. And
this perspective leads directly to the discussion of areas of contestation

---

[8] See my analysis of a passage from *The Busconductor Hines* in 'Alien Voices from the Street:
Demotic Modernism in Modern Scots Writing', in *The Yearbook of English Studies*, 25 : 'Non-
standard Englishes and the new media' (Modern Humanities Research Association, 1995), 141–
55 (pp. 147–8). See also the writing in *Not Not While the Giro*, with its echoes of Beckett.
[9] My thanks go to Alastair Renfrew for letting me read a draft of his paper, exchanged during
our correspondence, December 1995.

in wider questions of cultural challenge, literary expectation and critical practice. Once situated in this field, Kelman's demotic narrational
voice (however much it plays in a single register) cannot help but foreground (and hence perhaps deconstruct) the prevailing norm and the
authority of that long tradition of educated narrational discourse which
he has called the 'standard third party narrative voice':

> [...] the one that most people don't think of as a 'voice' at all—
> except maybe the voice of God—and they take for granted that it is
> unbiased and objective. But it's no such thing. Getting rid of that
> [...] is getting rid of a whole value system. You have to start exam-
> ining every term. The example I would use is the terms 'beautiful',
> or 'pretty', or 'handsome', or 'ugly'. There is no possibility of using
> such a term in my work, not in the standard narrative, it's not a
> possibility [...] This is an extreme example of the kind of formal
> problems you might have to get through; in a way to begin a story
> from nothing.[10]

The connection, as Kelman sees it, between poetics and politics could
not be more clearly put, nor his determination to carry forward the
contestation of literary authority, as his Booker speech would have
made even more clear, had the television medium allowed him time to
deliver it complete. (There's another debate to be held over all the little
suppressions which present themselves as no more than the neutral
technical imperatives of the medium itself.) Kelman's full text, for example, called on the Nigerian experience of Achebe, Soyinka and Tu-
tuola and of Ngugi in Kenya, as fellow writers facing what he takes to
be similarly monological value systems.

The Booker prize is cited advisedly, along with the silly correspondence that raged for a while about how many times the fuck word appeared in Kelman's novel (one eident reader proposed 4,000 citations).
However trivial, such signals serve to confirm the point that in the
public eye, and in the forum of literary production and publication,
Scottish writers are increasingly being seen as self-consciously politicised harbingers and proponents of just this kind of challenge to cultural authority, literary convention and common decorum.

In a recent article, the literary agent Robin Robertson (first at Secker
& Warburg and now at Jonathan Cape) was described as having
scooped the pool of the most exciting new writers in Britain, resolutely

---

[10] Kirsty McNeill, 'Interview with James Kelman', *Chapman*, 57 (Summer 1989), 4.

anti-metropolitan and un-middle class, and the most daring of these voices from the youth jungle and/or the urban wasteland were hailed as coming from Scotland, starting of course, with Kelman himself.[11] The term 'gritty urban realism' has been heard in the land (to muffled screams from all thinking readers, not to mention the writers themselves) and Alan Warner, Duncan McLean, Gordon Legge, Janice Galloway, Agnes Owen, Jeff Torrington and of course Irvine Welsh are being written about as if they were a 'movement'. (In this public forum, and *à propos* the visual media in particular, there's a whole different study to be made on what the film adaptation of *Trainspotting* has done to modulate and perhaps even to defuse the genuinely confrontational aspects of that text.)

For present purposes it is neither necessary nor fruitful to debate how accurate this popular perception is, but rather to register its presence, and to touch once again on Scottish literature's long standing engagement (for complex social, linguistic and historical reasons) with Rabelaisian excess, referred to in my opening summary as the Christis Kirk tradition of 'dancing and deray' carried through Ramsay, Fergusson, Burns, Hogg, William Tennant, MacDiarmid, Goodsir Smith, Alasdair Gray et al. It is indeed possible to argue that if a demotic and democratic strain can be identified in the new young writers named above, then the model of Rabelaisian energy is equally present in their work. But what we have established as a particularly Scottish penchant for Rabelaisian excess may now be coming back to haunt us in unexpected and uncomfortable ways—and it should be uncomfortable, for surely the whole point of inversion and travesty is that they be deeply disturbing and indeed subversive to fundamental and treasured value systems? The true force of carnival must be more than a passing breach of middle-class 'good taste'.

I suggest that it is against this Bakhtinian context that we must re-examine and try to evaluate (for better or for worse) the punk street energy in the writing of Gordon Legge, Duncan McLean and Irvine Welsh, or the celebration of tough-minded, amoral female independence in Alan Warner's *Morvern Callar*.[12] Or Janice Galloway's out-

---

[11] Catherine Lockerbie, 'Pole Position', *The Weekend Scotsman*, 10 June, 1995, 6–9. Readers may like to reflect on the implications of the implied reference to Mario Puzo and the Mafia, on the front cover of *The Weekend Magazine* which showed a moody portrait of Robertson with the heading 'Is this man the Godfather of Scottish literature?'

[12] The eponymous hero of *Morven Callar* appropriates her dead boyfriend's novel as her own at the beginning of the book and makes a literary reputation by it, even although she is resolutely unliterary herself. I think that the larger structural significance of this act is to establish a very

standing exploration of mental breakdown, male institutional authority and female 'hysteria' in *The Trick is to Keep Breathing*.

Then there is Irvine Welsh's notorious celebration of drug culture in the housing schemes of Edinburgh, and an analysis of this writing may well lead us to reappraise in turn our own understanding of carnivalia and Rabelaisian excess, and to think again (perhaps in less comfortable terms) about what such excess represents, should it be translated into immediately contemporary and secular terms. I can think of no more graphic recognition of the grossness of the body, its grotesque appetites, and our enslavement to the world of physical and material desire and being than, say, the now notorious opium suppository episode in *Trainspotting*. This passage is rich in anal and fecal references and indeed there are many other images of appetite, excretion and menstruation throughout the text. At the most basic level these reminders of food and reproduction are exactly what our consumer society—despite its deeply materialistic and hedonistic foundations—will not confront and can only rarely express. Consider for example, Nina's menstruation; Hazel's serving of tomato soup and coffee in the restaurant; or the Houston family and the shitty sheets. There is a barely disguised element of infantile glee in the comedy of such scenes, and Welsh is not entirely innocent of what some readers will see as an ultimately childish need to shock. But it's worth reflecting that 'shit' is a familiar synonym for heroin, and that drug addiction is an extraordinarily effective trope for the most primitive drives of the infant appetite, including its cloacal obsessions. The drug cycle may well be connected to our infantile desires for the bliss of fullness and the subsequent repression of a responsible self; to a desire for no less than extinction (however temporary) followed by the inevitable and painful return to life, appetite and reborn need. Welsh's characters demonstrate a Rabelaisian cycle of feeding, death and resurrection no less grotesque and excessive than the more traditional rituals of *carne vale*.

In Welsh's underculture the highs and lows of heroin addiction become a still wider social and political trope for the passage of life-experience itself—especially if you posit that bourgeois society has nothing to offer these young men but the scrap heap in the first place. In this respect Welsh's 'Junk Dilemmas' might be said to have rewrit-

---

clear symbolic watershed between the familiar tropes of literary alienation in dozens of previous novels, and Morvern Callar's orientation towards the totally experiential moment, almost always through music, physical movement, rave culture and (in at least two senses of the word) ecstasy.

ten Beckett's *Waiting for Godot* in radical but no less urgent or compelling terms:

> *Junk Dilemmas No. 66*
>
> *It's a challenge tae move: but it shouldnae be. Ah can move. It has been done before. By definition, we, humans, likes, are matter in motion. Why move anyway, when you have everything you need right here. Ah'll soon huv tae move though. Ah'll move when ah'm sick enough; ah know that through experience as well. Ah jist cannae conceive ay ever being that sick that ah'll want tae move. This frightens me, because ah'll need tae move soon.*
>
> *Surely ah'll be able tae dae it; surely tae fuck.*[13]

The 'bad' language and the strikingly working class presence of these characters takes them well out of the more familiar (and hence less challenging) genre of highbrow literary alienation and the minority hipster cultures of Left Bank or New York intellectuals described in the earlier writings of Alexander Trocchi or William Burroughs. The sexually radical, semi-criminal or racist underworlds evoked in the work of Genet or Céline may offer a closer fit to Welsh's territory, but here again their vision is of an under-world, when the focus of the Scottish writer's work seems to be to show the daylight reality of our common city streets. However extreme the junk-driven excesses of Welsh's characters might be, they are not offered as examples (generically comforting examples in the end) of isolated Dostoevskian 'extremity'. On the contrary, in Welsh's work the physical excesses of junk or violence or ecstatic release have become democratised and familiar, closely associated, moreover, with the traditionally working-class mass culture of football, or with common pub-culture, or with the crowded youth scenes at raves, all realised, it might be said, as visions of another kind of carnival.

There is not room in this essay for an extended discussion of what form 'carnival' might take in a modern secular civil society, when merely anti-clerical or other such transgressive postures have lost their power to challenge the roots of society and spiritual authority. But perhaps something of the older carnival spirit may yet be identified in the field of mass football culture and, beyond that again, in the atavistic

---

[13] Irvine Welsh, *Trainspotting* (London: Secker & Warburg, 1993), p. 177.

thrills—undoubtedly felt by significant numbers of young men—of partisan conflict, territorial boasting and ritualised fan violence.

If this seems too disturbing an extension of Bakhtin's concept of carnivalia, I would suggest that as modern readers we have tended to lose our sense of what was once truly disturbing in its classical or medieval manifestations. I would suggest, too, that we have tended to lose our sense of what Bakhtin saw as the early link between carnival and the novel genre itself—because of the form's once shocking social energy and its (now no longer remarkable) heterogenic and heteroglossial capacity. But today the voices from the housing estates and the rabid songs from the football terraces are being heard in the land of the popular novel—no longer the *des res* territory of a middle-class value system and its tribulations. The 'barbarians' are at the gates, and some of what they have to say is a much-needed reminder of subversive excess and suppressed energies. And some of it is genuinely barbaric.

Welsh's writing can be seen to be directly political in its expressions of contempt for a society and a social care system which seems to have failed what it would class as its 'less fortunate' or weaker members. In one way or another his characters are marked by fear, anger or genial indifference (sometimes all three) and we can empathise with their condition and its root causes. But at other times what they have to say seems to come from the deepest wells of infantile rage and resentment, an anti-social wound so deep that no humanly imaginable structure would ever be able to heal or help it.

Such a breach is indeed profound, and yet even this can generate its own politics of existential disaffection. Thus Welsh's accounts of football violence in *Marabou Stork Nightmares* take us beyond the established (and hence comforting) liberal and sociological scenarios of deprivation, to offer instead (or as well) an account of pure Nietzschean will in action. What Roy Strang celebrates is the 'rush' of physical violence and it is this sense of exhilaration and existential liberation which marks out 'most of the top boys', which is to say: 'it wasn't even bottle. It was not giving a fuck about anything'.[14] In Strang's world the old festivals of utopian misrule have mutated, or been reincarnated in the swirl of the football crowds and most especially in the ritually nihilistic confrontations between rival supporters. The paradox of his position is that Strang must remain anonymous in

---

[14] Irvine Welsh, *Marabou Stork Nightmares* (London: Jonathan Cape, 1995), p. 153. Subsequent page references are given in the text.

the eyes of the law while seeking notoriety in his own circles as an uninhibited fighter, and in this respect the law colludes with him, for he soon recognises that 'the polis werenae bothered too much aboot crimes against the person as long as you never bothered posh cunts or shoppers' (137). Carnival has always found its own space, and perhaps it has always involved a similarly uneasy compromise between licensed holiday and uncontrolled license. On a technical and linguistic level, there's no doubt that *Marabou Stork Nightmares* also generates intriguing satirical tensions between its working class demotic speech and the stilted public school diction of 'Boy's Own Paper' fiction along the lines of 'ripping yarns' in an imperial or colonial setting (for this is the form that is taken by protagonist Roy Strang's fantasy dreams as he lies in hospital in a coma). And the novel sets this category of discourse against the more directly historical experience of the appallingly dysfunctional Strang family as recent emigrants to South Africa, where young Roy recognises black oppression and is sexually abused in his turn by a racist uncle. In this respect the narrative layers and styles of the novel are much richer and more multiple than was the case in *Trainspotting*. Yet this polyphony is still deeply inscribed in powerlessness, the ultimate powerlessness, self-contempt and evasiveness of the racially, culturally and/or sexually abused. Whether it manifests itself along psychological, socio-linguistic or political fault lines, the end result of such a sense of powerlessness is very clearly shown to be violence, homophobia, the most profound sexism, male rage and rape. All symbolised indeed by the self-hating paralysis of Strang's coma (which lasts throughout the novel) and the plot's conclusion in castration.

Is it entirely a coincidence, I ask myself, that these images of public disorder, male rage, social failure and the horrors of the self-destructive will should arise in contemporary Scottish writing, as if they were the nightmare re-visiting of an older and prouder tradition of demotic difference and the self-validating, anti-hierarchical energy, inversion and liberation (however temporary) of Rabelaisian carnival? On the other hand, if the low society of carnival represents everything that bourgeois culture and state authority must repress or cannot bear to face, then we may well ask whether Irvine Welsh's world is not also truly, frighteningly, carnivalesque? Or, at the very least, we might see it as no less than legitimate expression from the mouths of those who have been denied any other form of discourse but the carnivalesque. Such questions may well lead us to re-examine a generally uncritical acceptance and perhaps a too comfortable validation of the Rabelaisian strain in Scottish literature; and they may lead us to reconsider, too, what carnival excess might actually look like in a modern, secular civil society—long separated from the pomp of the church and folk roots in food, feasting and organic renewal.

The best of Bakhtin's critical inheritance is to recognise the ethical and social significance of the multiple nature of discourses, and the conflict between them, and to recognise, too, how important it is that such contestation should be allowed to enter, or must force its way into the public forum and the canon of educated dialogue and 'serious' literature in order to change it, and to be changed in turn. The centrifugal and centripetal processes involved in this contest exist in a changing and dynamic relationship with each other; we make them, and they make us, which is why the questions raised here must be addressed and answered as best as we can, year by year. Even if the process cannot be closed, nor one tendency permanently privileged over the other; even if this paper does end, as it started, with a quintessentially monological voice:

> ...if I know not the meaning of the voice, I shall be unto him that speaketh a barbarian, and he that speaketh shall be a barbarian unto me.

Them and Us?
Representation of Speech in Contemporary Scottish Fiction

Alastair Renfrew

It is worth starting from the commonplace that any attempt to define a given culture must inevitably be dominated by the question of language, through which all other questions are refracted, or through which they must be forced. The literature of any culture, whose medium in the simplest sense language is, or, put another way, for which the centrality of the question of language is explicit, presents itself therefore as a compelling ground for such an attempt. In respect of what I will for the moment call linguistically 'peripheral' cultures, in which certain types of linguistic division are themselves more explicit, and in which the idea of language as essentially *dis*-unified is less likely to provoke dispute, the ground of literature becomes virtually irresistible. I propose, therefore, to work outwards from an examination of certain representations of speech in recent Scottish fiction towards a preliminary consideration of certain of the cultural representations they may imply.

One

The work of Tom Leonard, although substantially in verse, nonetheless provides a perfect means of both introducing and underwriting the issues I want to discuss in relation to fiction. Leonard writes in what is sometimes called 'phonetic urban dialect', a phonetically imitative orthography designed to render as directly as possible a Glasgow dialect speech. Leonard explicitly contests what is at once myth and intellectual orthodoxy: that in the beginning there was the word. Instead there was sound, or what Robert Frost, inhabiting the territory somewhere between myth and intellectual orthodoxy, argued poetry should take as its object: 'the speaking tone of voice somehow entangled in the words and fastened to the page for the ear of the imagination'.[1] The following lines from 'Unrelated Incidents (3)' display Leonard's divergent orthography, and perhaps the definitive end to which it is put:

> thirza right
> way ti spell
> ana right way

---

[1] Robert Frost, *Selected Prose*, ed. by Hyde Cox and Edward Connery Lathem (New York: Macmillan, 1968), pp. 13–14.

ti tok it.this
is me tokn yir
right way a
spellin.this
is ma trooth.[2]

Regardless of his acknowledged debt to William Carlos Williams, and a temptation to interpret his characteristic forbearance of rhyme and metrical regularity in terms of an unproblematic 'Modernism', Leonard's form seems designed to ensure that nothing detracts from or obscures the image of speech itself; he constructs a space which privileges the oral to an almost unsurpassable degree. It has become the new article of faith of Scottish criticism to connect such specific characteristics of individual writers with a 'national preference for the speech act (as a guarantee of some sort of authenticity) over the written text, even if that speech act is, paradoxically, written down'.[3] It is with what this formulation elides that I will be principally concerned, that is, with what Frost's dictum at least acknowledges in its inclusion of the problematic 'somehow'. Leonard's verse negotiates the transposition of speech into writing with the minimal transformation of the object in the process of its representation. It self-consciously remains, however, *writing*, as the following example from Leonard's short story 'Honest' confirms:

> They'll probably say sumhm like, 'Doon thi road!', anif you say, 'What?' they usually say 'Down the road!' the second time—though no always. Course, they never really say, 'Doon thi road!' or 'Down the road!' at all. Least they never say it the way its spelt. Coz it izny spelt, when they say it, is it?[4]

When taking speech (or 'sound') as its object, the absolutely minimal transformation of such a writing can never quite become zero. In this sense, it is a *writing* degree zero, a perhaps ultimate refinement of referential illusionism.

The space between a purely nominal zero transformation of the object in the process of representation and the zero degree of writing can be illustrated with a further example from 'Honest', in which a dialect

[2] Tom Leonard, *Intimate Voices* (Newcastle: Galloping Dog Press, 1984), p. 88.
[3] Roderick Watson, 'Dialects of "Voice" and "Place": Literature in Scots and English from 1700', in Paul H. Scott (ed.), *Scotland: A Concise Cultural History* (Edinburgh & London: Mainstream, 1993), pp. 99–125.
[4] 'Honest', in *Intimate Voices*, pp. 72–75 (p. 73).

speaker's phonetically transcribed variant of the standard English 'it is not as if' is 'It's Noah's if ' (Leonard, 72). Here, as in the earlier example, Leonard plays with assumptions about the necessity of 'consistency' in his orthography, demonstrating not only that it is arbitrary rather than systematic, but also, and crucially, that the relationship of the oral to the written must *always be arbitrary*, must always involve transformation through choices which pertain only to writing. Another example, perhaps even more useful in that it doesn't involve representation of dialect speech, but rather polemically directed parody of so-called standard English speech, is Leonard's 'quotation' of a former teacher, who expressed her pride in sharing 'the byootiful lengwidge of Milton'.[5] An *oral* mimicry of such diction would amount to little more than a stale stereotyping, conveying nothing of the apparent divergence of standard English diction and standard English orthography, or, put another way, conveying nothing of the *equally arbitrary* nature of that orthography. Thus even an orthography which seems designed to efface the boundaries between speech and writing is in fact just another means by which the constancy of those boundaries is sign-posted.

The prose writing of James Kelman has also tended to receive attention primarily in terms of its relation to the oral, in terms of Kelman's ability to render the speech of a class of speaker customarily denied a 'voice' in literature. Roderick Watson has been prepared to take this approach to an extreme whereby Kelman's refusal to move outside the experiential sphere of his characters, allied to a narrative voice indistinguishable from 'the demotic utterances of [those] characters' permits him to render their experience '*without a trace of imitation* or condescension' ('Dialects of "Voice", etc.', 121; my emphasis). The issue of 'condescension' is inescapably evaluative, dependent on certain assumptions concerning the relationship of the real author to that aspect of the real world taken as his or her object, and hence need not concern us at present. The expression 'without a trace of imitation', however, tends to suggest that Kelman's writing is subject to the same assumptions regarding 'orality' that I have sought to dispel in relation to Leonard. Kelman is in fact far from the extreme control situation we encountered in Leonard's writing, and hence even further distanced from the illusion of zero transformation of the

---

[5] 'The Proof of the Mince Pie', *Intimate Voices*, pp. 65–71 (p. 65).

object in the process of its representation. On the basic level of orthography, Kelman is much less insistent on phonetic suggestiveness, raising
the question of whether a 'phonetic urban dialect' writing is sustainable
(or necessary) for much longer than the four pages of, for example,
Leonard's 'Honest'. Kelman is actually extremely close to a standard
English orthography, but this is only the point from which our differ-
entiation begins; the space between Leonard's near absolutism and Kelman is determined not simply by orthographies, but more profoundly by
the conflicting imperatives of their respective conceptions of speech as
object, and by the consequent imperatives of the particular forms they
employ. Kelman's prose narratives cannot simply rely on a formal affinity
with the terse, instantly defined real speech act in the way that Leonard's
verse can. The result would merely be a repetition of a primary vice of
much earlier Scottish fiction, the assignment of dialect only to the direct
speech of characters (and largely to 'low' or comic characters at that),
while the diegetic narrative remains standard English. As Watson and
others have pointed out, however, Kelman maintains a linguistic continuity between those sections of his novels dominated by character
speech, and those traditionally assigned to authorial voice. This is ach-
ieved by means of a concentration on *inner speech*, steadfastly identified
with the patterns of actual speech, and rendered in a free indirect form.
These 'interior monologues' are the centre of Kelman's own particular
referential illusionism, provoking the kind of assessment noted above, i.e.,
that the narrative voice becomes indistinguishable 'from the demotic
utterances of [the] characters'. This process of identification has been
gradual and constant in Kelman's work, and its most concentrated manifestation has thus come in his most recent novel, *How late it was, how
late*. I want first to give an example of the power of this technique,
followed by a couple which I hope will illustrate its limits:

> no too big a stride, but enough, just enough, to keep going and ye get
> yerself into something or other yer head just gets full of it it just gets
> full of it, full of that and nothing but the truth man that's how it goes,
> that is the truth and it is nothing but the truth, nothing but the truth, ye
> feel a wee space and it's only a doorway only a doorway and a wee bit
> in the dark and yer hands feeling fuck all for a couple of wee bits and
> then there, there it is there, the next wall, just after the doorway and

> now okay, thank fuck he had had a breakfast, the sodjers giving him a
> breakfast [] right, on ye go, a hearty hi yo silver[6]

Here outward evidence of authorial presence is restricted to the third
person 'he' in the second last line, by which time it has become virtually
impossible to register it in the third person at all. It functions merely as a
trace, marking the point at which the reader's perspective on distinct
sources of narration all but merges.

> His belly was fucking in knots man telling ye.   (43)

In this instance, however, the relationship between authorial and character
speech has become much more clearly one of balance, even tension:
Sammy's physical condition is related in a construction which strongly
suggests direct address ('telling ye'), but that construction is at least
formally initiated in the third person. Authorial and character speech may
be locked into a single utterance, but they are clearly delineated nonetheless. This gradual separation is complete in the following:

> One thing about the Sammy fellow, a fucking battler. If ye had asked
> him he would have telt ye: nay brains but he would aye battle like fuck.
> It's true though he would have a go.   (47)

Despite the explicit third person reference not just to Sammy, but to the
'Sammy fellow', the first part of this is the same kind of construction as
those we have already seen, in which the perspectives and diction of
author and character merge. The second part, however, appears to be pure
authorial speech, an example of the narrative voice assenting to the
content of another point of view, but at the same time explicitly distancing
itself from the hyperbolic and agitated means of expression of that point of
view, an expression which is authored by Sammy himself. At this point
author and character stand apart, and the illusion of their 'indistinguishable' voices is shattered.

This process of mapping out the space between Kelman's writing and
the speech which is its principal object would be usefully continued

---

[6] James Kelman, *How late it was, how late* (London: Secker & Warburg, 1994), p. 50. Subsequent
page references are given in the text.

through the full range of his narrative techniques,[7] but it has been my
purpose only to establish, by assessing Kelman in relation to the datum set
by Leonard's verse, something of the nature of that space, and to suggest
that criticism must aim at its reconstitution, rather than to surmount or
elide it.

A particularly powerful contribution to such a reconstitution, in as much
as it comprises a specific theorization of the relation of speech and
writing, is Bakhtin's theory of speech genres. Bakhtin proposes a unified
model of discourse, the various spheres of which are distinguished by
their own characteristic types of utterances, or speech genres, but which
are nonetheless unified by their 'common *verbal* (linguistic) nature' (PSG,
61; trans. modified). An essential unity is therefore implied between
language used in literary and non-literary locations, a unity which is at
least provisionally fractured by Bakhtin's institution of a more productive
distinction, that between primary (or simple) and second-order (or
complex) speech genres, the latter arising 'in conditions of more complex
and relatively highly developed cultural intercourse' (PSG, 62; trans.
modified). Such intercourse will tend, crucially, to be written rather than
oral, and to be socio-political, scientific or artistic in nature. What is of
particular interest in the present context is Bakhtin's precise description of
the mechanics of the second-order speech genres:

> In the process of their formation they absorb into themselves and re-
> work various primary (simple) genres, which arose in conditions of
> direct verbal intercourse. These primary genres, on entering into the
> structure of the complex, are transformed and acquire a particular
> character: they lose their direct relation to [reality] and to the real
> utterances of others; for example, a [sample] of domestic dialogue or a
> letter in a novel, while preserving its form and domestic meaning only
> on the plane of the content of the novel, enters into actual reality only
> through the novel as a whole, that is as a literary-artistic event and not
> one of domestic life. (PSG, 62; trans. modified).

In this sense, a second-order genre like the novel is formed out of the vast
diversity of primary genres (and from other second-order genres); the
principle of construction is not, however, one of straightforward assembly,
but rather of what we might call transformative incorporation. The
primary genres, which are formed in the course of direct, actual inter-

---

[7] See in this connection Roderick Watson's 'Alien Voices from the Street: Demotic Modernism
in Modern Scots Writing', in *The Yearbook of English Studies*, 25: 'Non-standard Englishes and
the New Media' (Modern Humanities Research Association, 1995), 141–55.

action between people and social groups across the full range of human contact, are *re-used* in the formation of the second-order genres.

Although Bakhtin is addressing the formation of genres, which should provoke our caution in proceeding directly to consideration of individual works, we can at least consider the individual work as participating in this process of exchange between patterns of speech and the shape of literature. The individual novel is as much a whole, albeit complex, utterance as even the briefest snippet of dialogue which is reproduced (transformed) in it (PSG, 62). As such, the individual novel, as much as any other utterance, 'participates in the "unitary language" (in its centripetal forces and tendencies) and at the same time partakes of social and historical heteroglossia (the centrifugal, stratifying forces)' (DN, 272). The utterance itself (in this case an entire novel) is in other words both the location and the agent of generic change. It should prove extremely worthwhile, then, to review our earlier remarks on the representations of Leonard and Kelman in the light of the idea that the types of verbal material of their work have been formed over an indeterminate period, largely outwith the literary domain, their outlines emerging out of a process of constant evolution in actual verbal interaction, and that it is precisely these types which are selected and represented in the literary work. What may have been a whole utterance 'in life', identified with its own particular genre of speech, becomes a *re-accentuated* component of a whole literary utterance, which is in turn identified with a particular second-order genre. Insistence upon an approach that confronts the relationship of speech and writing specifically in terms of representation does not necessarily imply an absolute insistence on Bakhtin's particular model, which is itself only a proposed context in which to view representation of speech. Bakhtin's model does, however, offer a crucial advantage: although it asserts the inevitability of transformation of language as an object of representation, its prescription for that transformation preserves the unity of primary and second-order uses of language, and thus potentially preserves the unity of speech and writing. This in a sense obviates the kind of criticism which focuses on 'orality' in Kelman and Leonard, because that criticism essentially seeks *redress* of a perceived tendency to devalue orality, and Bakhtin grants that 'redress' almost as a first principle.

Two

The category of speech genres has not been brought to bear on the
linguistic tensions of Scottish writing, but the concept which it is in a
sense an attempt to organise, that of heteroglossia, has been increasingly
invoked. Since David Morris saw in heteroglossia a vehicle for reparation
of the 'scandalous neglect' into which Burns's work had fallen, Bakhtin's
model of the social stratification of language has promised a new context
within which to interpret what Sydney Goodsir Smith, putting a particular
slant on a phenomenon which has occupied most commentators, called
'the linguistic split which has dogged Scottish literature'.[8] The attractions
of Bakhtin's absolute refutation of the idea of any national language as
unitary are clear in respect of a literature whose medium has consistently
appeared to be a language within a language; these attractions are more
sharply focused in the light of Bakhtin's alternative conception of
language as a dynamic, constantly evolving system, stratified into overlapping and interactive languages of social groupings, professions, generations, and of course into dialects. Further, this model is not nearly so
appropriate to the terms of Scottish literature's linguistic split which
pertained in the eighteenth and nineteenth centuries, and for most of the
twentieth, as it is at present. The language of Scottish Literature was
previously characterised by a series of resistances to the steadily
increasing influence of English, each of which sought to *reconstruct* a
viable and distinct literary medium from whichever sources were
available. These sources included dialect elements and earlier literary
exemplars, but a cycle of revival and neglect, with each revival feeding off
increasingly hybrid sources, essentially resulted in a situation where the
literary alternative to English could not be identified even vaguely with a
language that anyone actually spoke. This is of course true to a certain
extent of any writing, but that should not obscure the fact that we can no
longer (if indeed we ever could) speak of a single linguistic division with
regard to Scottish writing. The examples we have looked at, and indeed
the broad movement towards dialect writing of which they are a part,

---

[8] David Morris, 'Burns and Heteroglossia', in *The Eighteenth Century: Theory and Interpretation*,
28.1 (1987), 3–27; Sydney Goodsir Smith, *A Short Introduction to Scottish Literature* (Serif, 1951),
p. 22. Morris's significantly positive article provoked, if not a flood, then certainly a steady stream of
material which has sought (mostly) to exploit Bakhtin as a particularly appropriate extension of the
sparse native theoretical tradition of G. Gregory Smith and MacDiarmid (and as a response to the
'counter-tradition' of Edwin Muir). Notable among these are: Carol McGuirk's 'Response to David
Morris' (see note 9); Robert Crawford's *Identifying Poets: Self and Territory in Twentieth-Century
Poetry* (Edinburgh: Edinburgh University Press, 1993), and the same author's 'Bakhtin and Scotlands', in *Scotlands*, 1 (1994), 55–65; and Roderick Watson's 'Dialects of "Voice" and "Place"' (see
note 3).

point to a concern with, specifically, the language that people speak; or, and this is a point to which we will return, with the *many languages* that people speak. Carol McGuirk, taking Bakhtin at his word as it were, has made the point that if *all* language is stratified throughout, then the particular line of division between Scots and English can be of no greater significance than any other, and might be argued to be considerably less vital than stratification in terms of gender or generation or class.[9] The simply conceived historical division (which could itself be redefined from the point of view of a heteroglot language) is best seen simply as a literary given, a persistent characteristic of the tradition against which recent writers are partially defined. As such it functions as a fault line, over which are laid more complex and *socially located* divisions, the literary traces of which we have begun to see.

The problem we must confront in raising the question of heteroglossia is not that of exhaustive description of the socially determined languages available to Scottish writers, but rather the extent to which this posited diversity has in fact penetrated their writing. Heteroglossia is given as a social fact, not as a literary property. Bakhtin not only discusses social heteroglossia as a concept or category, but also, and crucially, the specific formal means by which heteroglossia may enter the work (DN, 301–31); it is this penetration which facilitates the dialogization of the work, its formal organisation as a dialogue of diverse languages. It is in this sense that Bakhtin has been most widely deployed in literary studies, as a means by which the relationship of certain formal techniques to their linguistic 'cargo' can be interrogated in pursuit of their dialogic 'output'. It would be pointless to embark upon the systematic identification of instances of 'dialogism' in recent Scottish fiction, not least (if not only) because such a project might be carried out with a degree of success in respect of any body of writing; it is far more relevant to attempt to differentiate broad categories of such penetration of the literary work by social heteroglossia, and to address the growing assumption that the presence or even preponderance of dialect in itself constitutes 'diversity of speech'.

Kelman's *How late it was, how late* is dominated, as we have seen, by the inner speech of its main character, interlocked in a controlling narrative voice. The novel's direct speech, like its narrative, is dominated by dialect: even the extended dialogues between Sammy and the police

---

[9] Carol McGuirk, 'Burns, Bakhtin, and the Opposition of Poetic and Novelistic Discourse: A Response to David Morris', *The Eighteenth Century: Theory and Interpretation*, 32.1 (1991), 58–71.

are linguistically stable to the point where, unless vicious sarcasm be
admitted as a component of the socio-linguistic profile of the police, we
can only conclude that Sammy's (authoritarian, oppressive) tormentors
speak the *same language* as he does. The novel is in fact characterised by
the antithesis of diversity of speech. With the proviso once again that *How
late* is a particularly concentrated example of Kelman's work, it is fair to
say that the dominance of an essentially unitary voice is a recurrent
characteristic, perhaps even an ultimate aim. It is also necessary to note
that, just as Leonard marks an extreme in Scottish writing as a whole,
Kelman occupies that position with regard to fiction. His striving for the
pure, single voice, for the eventual concealment, perhaps, of referential
illusionism with regard to speech, is not so evident in other current writers
of fiction. Irvine Welsh's recent *Trainspotting* is narrated in several
voices, each of which, although broadly sharing a dialect, is modulated by
particularity of concern and, crucially, through their continual juxta-
position.[10] Each narrative voice is in its turn 'infected' by various forms
of parodic speech mimicry, and by the genre-specific lexis of drug and
football culture. The most striking instance of this is Spud's magnificent
hybrid of Edinburgh dialect and U.S. hep-cat jive-talk (imported,
presumably, from another, idealised 'drug culture'). The significance of
this diversity of narrative point of view in *Trainspotting* for the production
of a genuine diversity of speech is confirmed in comparison with the more
recent *Marabou Stork Nightmares*, in which the narration is split between
the 'different states' of the comatose Roy Strang.[11] Here the registers of
speech which respectively govern each narrative 'state' (dialect on the
one hand, and a parodic, highly stylised 'standard English' on the other)
are merely contrasted, set in simple opposition. Jeff Torrington's *Swing
Hammer Swing!* also evinces a community of subtly differentiated
speakers, each of which speaks a *variant* of a recognisable 'whole'
Glasgow dialect according to age, gender and 'class' (or 'micro-class').[12]
Here again, however, the narrative point of view is consistent (although
this is by no means an absolute nor even necessarily significant
impediment to diversity of speech), and the speakers' further dif-
ferentiation is limited and perhaps obviated by the novel's setting in the

---

[10] Irvine Welsh, *Trainspotting* (London: Secker & Warburg, 1993). It would perhaps be naive to
speculate as to the motivation for the effacement of dialect elements in the lamentable film version of
Trainspotting, which led, among many other things, to the spectacle of Renton delivering his open air
monologue on Scotland's 'cultural degradation/colonization' in a diction determined by the anticipated
'tolerance' of audiences beyond Scotland.
[11] Irvine Welsh, *Marabou Stork Nightmares* (London: Jonathan Cape, 1995).
[12] Jeff Torrington, *Swing Hammer Swing!* (London: Secker & Warburg, 1992).

comfortably mythical not-too-distant past. Both *Swing Hammer Swing!* and, in particular, *Trainspotting* are some way from the monologism of *How late it was, how late*; both are, however, marked by a dominance of the image of one particular socially located language, or at least of a group of closely related languages, and only *Trainspotting* could be argued to approach Bakhtin's definition of the dialogized novel, penetrated by 'social heteroglossia' or 'shot through' with diverse speech forms.

The citation of Janice Galloway's *The Trick Is To Keep Breathing* in this connection involves something of a paradox.[13] The controlling narrative voice seems designed to counterbalance another of the accusations laid at Kelman's door, i.e., that he effectively *characterises* the speaker for whom he 'provides' a 'voice' as male, aggressive, oppressed/repressed. Galloway's Joy is female and passive, characteristics which are virtually annihilated, in one way or another, by circumstances set in train by the death of a lover. The paradox is that Galloway's closure of the narrative in a single voice, a voice which is consistently resistant to the diversity of speech patterns by which any single 'voice' is inevitably surrounded, places the novel closer to Kelman than any of those cited above.

There is another kind of paradox in that the work of Alasdair Gray, who of all current Scottish prose writers seems least concerned with the question of dialect or 'non-standard' English, might be argued to be marked with the greatest degree of diversity of speech; crucial in this is the broad compositional technique of telling his 'stories' (at least) *twice*, though a more sophisticated analysis of Gray's compositional techniques might be mounted from the starting point of Bakhtin's concentration on parody, stylization and inserted genres among the compositional forms which permit the penetration into the novel of social heteroglossia.[14]

I want to argue, then, that the simple association of 'non-standard' speech forms with a heteroglot, dialogized literature is utterly misleading; it is further possible to argue that such a straightforward association masks only another form of *homogenisation* of language, a homogenisation

---

[13] Janice Galloway, *The Trick Is To Keep Breathing* (Edinburgh: Polygon, 1989).
[14] See for example Alasdair Gray, *Lanark* (Edinburgh; Canongate, 1981) and *Poor Things* (London: Bloomsbury, 1992). Gray's desultory rendition of various regional dialects in *Something Leather* (London: Jonathan Cape, 1990) can be read as parodic not of the speech forms themselves, but of the practice and techniques of their representation in fiction.

which defines the works which bear its mark as particularly limited
'utterances' in a broader cultural dialogue. It might be argued that the
individual writer contributes his or her particular 'strand' to a broader
diversity of speech, which is hence dependent more on a desired diversity
in the multiplicity of subjects writing (see the comparison of Kelman and
Galloway above); this is certainly consistent with the avowed (and
perhaps provisional) aim of Kelman, i.e., the reclamation of what, in terms
of voice, is constituted by the 'literary' (although this is also to accord too
fully with the expectation of a single voice from a single writer). It is,
however, difficult to see where the work of Kelman, although at the most
fundamental level clearly indicative of an important instability in the
language(s) spoken in Scotland, is capable of broadening out into
something more than a contribution to a simplistic, two-sided cultural
'debate'. The target in that 'debate' is the English language which has
constrained and restrained the language of Scottish writing, and English
culture in general, the 'dominant' culture to which the Scottish has been
peripheral. On this level Kelman makes an outraged retort to the likes of
Woolf, who strove after the inner speech of only a certain class of
speaker, apparently untroubled by the glaring contrast between the 'flux
of consciousness' of those and they, and the exchange of commonplaces
between the ciphers who people the fringes of her novels: in *To The
Lighthouse*, for example, the lengthy interior monologue of Mrs.
Ramsay's English speaking, six-year old son precedes a local Scots-
woman's characterisation of *her* own son, which is limited to the
staggeringly penetrative observation that he is 'a quiet one'. If Kelman is
participating in any kind of dialogue, then it is a straightforward
confrontational dialogue, between explicitly verbalised indignation on the
one side, and an inferred, virtually mute indifference on the other. The
complaint of the current article is not *in any sense* with the idea of a
dialect writing; indeed the Scottish tradition's tendency to resist dialect in,
specifically, the *prose genres* would seem to be the most pressing of
issues in any reconstruction of that tradition. The problem is that the
presence of dialect and the extension of what is deemed to be 'literary',
rather than being welcomed and analysed in comparison to the former
dearth and limitation respectively, have often been exaggerated as re-
presenting a diversity which non-dialect writing somehow necessarily
lacks. The novel is defined for Bakhtin in terms of its ability to absorb and
interanimate images of the full diversity of speech types which constitute a
'national' language at any point in its development. This social hetero-

glossia, which surrounds any writer located in any tradition, is transmuted in Kelman into a literary and cultural *schizoglossia*.[15]

Donald Wesling, in a direct comparison of elements of Scottish and Afro-Caribbean British writing, has enlisted terms used by James Clifford to distinguish different types of peripheral culture: Scottish culture meets the definition of a 'border' culture, having developed in a complex relationship of identification and distinction from the English culture to which it is directly contiguous; Afro-Caribbean British, on the other hand, is a 'diaspora' culture, partially defined by its former colonial relationship to the culture in the midst of which it is currently defining itself.[16] The latter of these, the 'diaspora' culture, is figured as a culture more profoundly involved in the process of its own formation; even more significantly, the discourse of the diaspora culture, to borrow yet another term, lies unequivocally *outside power*, bestowing upon that culture a greater degree of integral unity, a unity which is both earned and protected by strategies of *resistance*, as opposed to dialogue. The fiction of James Kelman (and, significantly, the polemic which has marked its reception) amounts to a misappropriation of the strategies appropriate to the unified 'resistance' culture; it too seeks to 'fend off the voices and registers of dominant discourse as unworthy dialogic partners' (Wesling, 320), rather than engaging with the *many* voices within Scottish culture, and beyond it. Scottish criticism, perhaps distracted by an atavism of the former 'single' linguistic division in Scottish writing, has tended to sanction this misrepresentation.

To misrepresent Scottish culture's relation to the 'dominant' culture to which it has been peripheral is not, however, merely a neutral exercise of wishful thinking, but has the unacceptable consequence of misrepresenting its relation to other 'peripheral' cultures. The orientation of Scottish writing within a loose 'postcolonial' framework might be enabling in many respects, but the (not unreasonable) price of this must be a recognition of the fact that the situation of the other cultures within that framework will substantially differ from our own, that each individually defined linguistic culture stands (and has long stood) in a substantively

---

[15] To borrow a term from the Scots lexicographer, John M. Kirk: 'The Heteronomy of Scots with Standard English', in *The Nuttis Schell: Essays on the Scots Language*, ed. by Caroline Macafee & Iseabail Macleod (Aberdeen: Aberdeen University Press, 1987), pp. 166–81.
[16] Donald Wesling, 'Mikhail Bakhtin and the Social Poetics of Dialect', in *Papers on Language and Literature*, 29.3 (1993), 303–22.

different position relative to the 'centre' of colonial power. Otherwise we are left to defend the indefensible implication that the Scots 'are bonded in comparable suffering with the wretched of the earth'.[17] Welsh explicitly raises, without ever resolving, this problem in *Marabou Stork Night-mares*, in the spectacle of a working-class Scottish family emigrating to the 'promised land' of a still white South Africa, only to meet with a variety of the 'abuse' endemic in that society. The absurdity of the 'bonded' Scot is, however, unequivocally, and ironically, illustrated in the Edinburgh dialect of Welsh's *Trainspotting*, complaining about the speakers of a dialect spoken little more than half-an-hour away on the train:

> Still, ah'm in nae shape tae argue, n even if a wis, it's pointless wi Weedjies [Glaswegians]. Ah've never met one Weedjie whae didnae think that they are the only genuinely suffering proletarians in Scotland, Western Europe, the World. Weedjie experience ay hardship is the only experience ay it. (191)

This is true, of course, only in fiction.

Andrew Noble, Letter to *The Daily Telegraph*, 14th. Oct. 1994.

Bakhtin and the Postcolonial Condition

Graham Pechey

> Science (and cultural consciousness) of the nineteenth century sin-
> gled out only a miniature world (and we have narrowed it even
> more) from the boundless world of literature. This miniature world
> included almost nothing of the East. The world of culture and litera-
> ture is essentially as boundless as the universe. We are speaking not
> about its geographical breadth (this is limited), but about its seman-
> tic depths, which are as bottomless as the depths of matter. The in-
> finite diversity of interpretations, images, figurative semantic com-
> binations, materials and their interpretations, and so forth. We have
> narrowed it terribly by selecting and by modernizing what has been
> selected. We impoverish the past and do not enrich ourselves. We
> are suffocating in the captivity of narrow and homogeneous inter-
> pretations (N70, 140).

If there is nothing new about the collocation in my title—of Bakhtin
and the postcolonial—this does not mean that there is nothing new to
be said about it. Biography may seem banal; it is none the less one
place to start; and it can be of positive benefit if we think of Bakhtin's
life at once in a global context and in the chronotopic (that is: spatio-
temporally situated) terms that he has himself taught us to apply to all
narratives. I will begin therefore in a literal, historical, biographically
focused idiom.

Mikhail Mikhailovich Bakhtin grew up in the metropolitan centre of
a vast empire of adjacent territories stretching unbroken between two
continents, and his lifespan covered that relatively short time between
the height of direct European imperial rule over the world and the post-
war decolonisation which brought at least a formal end to that global
hegemony. The last of the European empires, that of Portugal, crum-
bled only months before his death. What then of Bakhtin's 'own'
(Russian) empire? Though few, I think, would now claim that the
revolution which took place when he was twenty-two constituted a
process of decolonisation in anything more than the short term, it is
nevertheless the case that Lenin's teaching of the 'right of nations to
self-determination' committed the new Soviet order to a sponsorship of
such processes in other places. Class-based analysis was modified to
accommodate the aspirations of emergent nations, and an exotic plant
called the 'national bourgeoisie' was found to have excellent properties abroad, even if its counterpart nearer home (in, say, the Ukraine)
was rooted out as a noxious weed. 'Imperialism' was given a purely

economic meaning as a phase in the development of capitalism, and
was therefore inapplicable to a polity and economy that were suppos-
edly socialist. Under Stalin's rule, the political principle of 'proletarian
internationalism' (that code by which Soviet foreign policy compelled
all of its twists and turns into a transcendental coherence) went along
with a policy in the cultural field that denounced 'rootless cosmopol-
itanism': another code, by which was meant any aesthetic experiment
or *avant-garde* anti-aesthetic, any 'formalist' distraction from a muscu-
lar localism of content.

Bakhtin's attitude towards this sophistic legitimation of Stalinist ter-
ror masquerading as dialectics can only be inferred from the sub-text of
his writing, principally that which springs from his middle period. In
the Rabelais book, and in the great essays of that phase, he may be
seen to be using realist and populist language against the official aesthetics and politics usually carried by just such language. Celebrating
cross-cultural fertilisation and a hypertrophy of textuality in a writer of
early European modernity was a safe way of encoding a rejection of
chauvinism and a narrow aesthetic, while at the same time seeming to
speak only from the secure disciplinary haven of literary-historical
scholarship: close enough to the ground, as it were, not to seem to be
at odds with the official philosophy. It is only with his return to direct
philosophising in the Khrushchev 'thaw' that we find Bakhtin, even if
only in private jottings, developing a hermeneutics with clear ontological pretensions, theorizing meaning as such and inflecting his investigation towards the question of being. Interestingly, then, it is in these
late writings that we also find him using terms which allegorise the
typical experience of those whose fates have been shaped by empire:
experiences of exile, diaspora, migrancy; experiences that in the late
twentieth century have come to be specifically associated with the
condition called 'postcoloniality'. The story of meaning is for Bakhtin
a story of nomadism and (internal) exile much like his own, a story of
wandering under the aspect of an always-potential homecoming in that
dimension of semantic infinity-eternity which he calls 'great time'
(RQ, 4–5; MHS, 167–70).[1]

I will come back to this transcendental migrancy of meaning and its
relationship to historical experiences of postcoloniality later. In the
meantime I wish to bring out the distinction between my current sense

---

[1] See in this respect Graham Pechey, 'Eternity and Modernity: Bakhtin and the Epistemological
Sublime', in *Theoria* (1993), 61-85 (pp. 81–82).

of 'Bakhtin and the postcolonial' and earlier versions of the latter, including my own. Bakhtin's reception in the West as a 'poststructuralist before the letter' led inevitably to the drafting of some of his categories into the service of theories of the postcolonial; and no wonder, given that in some of the major writers in the field (Gayatri Spivak and Homi Bhabha, for example) we find the poststructuralism of the Western academy adding colonial discourse to its hit-list of worthy candidates for deconstruction. None the less, as Robert Young has shown, Bakhtin's proto-poststructuralism is not so much a fortuitous prolepsis as an effect produced by his presence at the very birth of the poststructuralist 'turn' in the 1960s, and most notably in the work of Julia Kristeva.[2] He it was who offered the key for those who wanted to escape from structuralism's 'prison-house of language'[3] into that broad hinterland of historicity that lies beyond the walled metropolis of systematicity, while still placing discourse in the foreground of their readings (Tzvetan Todorov is a peculiarly overt instance of this strategic recourse to Bakhtinian categories).[4] So it is that when the newest crop of postcolonial critics write of 'selving' and 'othering' and 'double-voicing' and the like, they are willy-nilly recycling at perhaps one or two removes a reach-me-down Bakhtinian vocabulary—and not always in a way that does justice to the tacit or acknowledged source of those expressions.

The trajectory of my own erstwhile *marxisant* poststructuralism led me at length to the postcolonial. I was then to find at the end of this aberrant though (as it now seems to me) still valuable tangent that the matter had been the other way round: that it was my colonial upbringing and my experience of exile which had made Bakhtin appeal to me in the first place. I first came across his work in 1971, when I was in South Africa on a home visit and (my South African citizenship having been stripped from me) contemplating what turned out to be a ten-year stint in the limbo of statelessness. Bakhtin's ideas fell on what I now can see to have been, in psychic terms, fertile ground for growth. Having then published my first short piece on Bakhtin back in England in 1980, I found myself in the peroration of an article of 1987 extending his categories of the text to the 'social text', and in particular using

---

[2] Robert Young, 'Back to Bakhtin', *Cultural Critique*, 2 (1985), 71–92.
[3] See Frederic Jameson, *The Prison-House of Language* (Princeton: Princeton University Press, 1972).
[4] See Tzvetan Todorov, *Mikhail Bakhtin: The Dialogical Principle* (Manchester: Manchester University Press, 1984).

apartheid as one of the most fascinating exemplary cases in our time of
a 'social' monologism, one that (like textual monologisms and cultural
monoglossias) needed always to be posited by a political act of will
against a dialogical and/or heteroglot reality.[5] In a piece published in
1990 I developed Bakhtin's idea of novelistic 'polyphony' as a metaphor for a functioning civil society, and (again in a polemical coda) I
turned to the colonial margins, locating Bakhtin's true successors in
the revolutionary intellectuals of those zones.[6] I read Frantz Fanon's
Black Skin, White Masks as a politically engaged incarnation of Bakhtin's dialogue of 'personalities' at odds with the classical dialectic
perpetuated (with whatever modifications) in the sympathetic writing
of metropolitan existentialism; and I read Paulo Freire's *Pedagogy of
the Oppressed*, with its call for 'dialogical cultural action', as an instance of dialogism in third-world revolutionary praxis. The early
1990s saw further published work in which I developed these ideas,
focusing more narrowly on South Africa (then in the last and most tur-
bulent phase of its liberation struggle) and turning more and more explicitly in a 'post-Marxist' direction.

Some other features of this work of mine need to be flagged up before we can move on. These are: first, its shift of interest from Bakhtin's work of the middle period and towards the earliest and the last
work (then appearing for the first time in English); and, secondly, the
recognition that the central categories of the middle period (dialogue,
novel, carnival) not only emphasised ambivalence in their objects but
were themselves shot through with ambivalence. It was thus that I
came to write 'Not the Novel: Bakhtin, Poetry, Truth, God', an essay
that sought to undo from the inside (as it were) Bakhtin's notorious
condescension towards the genres of poetry and drama, and to show
that these generic antitypes of the novel were not the disposable con-
venience that they seemed but both covertly integral to his overt preference for novelistic discourse and no less susceptible of theorization
in Bakhtinian terms.[7] Carnival and novel as categories were, I argued,
inwardly occupied by opposites or antecedents that they did not negate
but rather renewed, launched again under new conditions into history. I
suggested that we see poetry as a an 'old' (premodern) genre surviving

---

[5] Graham Pechey, 'On the borders of Bakhtin: dialogization, decolonisation', in *Bakhtin and
Cultural Theory*, ed. by Ken Hirschkop and David Shepherd (Manchester: Manchester University Press, 1989), pp. 39–67; first published in the *Oxford Literary Review* (1987).
[6] Graham Pechey, 'Boundaries versus Binaries: Bakhtin in/against the History of Ideas', *Radical
Philosophy*, 54 (1990), 23–31.
[7] Graham Pechey, 'Not the Novel: Bakhtin, Poetry, Truth, God', *Pretexts*, 4.2 (1993).

within modernity as a self-framing and self-contextualizing practice of writing which was no less authentic for being so: 'stylization' rather than 'style', and yet in a certain relation to truth; ironic and double-voiced under a novelizing influence, yet able also to reach into its generic memory for the language of praise and of the sublime. I suggested, finally, that this was easier to see if one took one's stand not in the European metropolis but in a situation that was (in a Hegelian phrase) 'world-historically' skewed, that did not follow the seemingly straightforward epochal 'timing' of modernity: in a (post)colonial context, for example.

Needless to say, South Africa was again my exemplary instance. Here was a place where the defining cultural and political forms of the modern world were to be found, in however distorted a form; but here also was a place where poetry was a mass experience; where primary and secondary oralities intersected in urban popular performance; where slogans and hymns and praise songs fired partisans of 'the struggle'; and where the charisma and auratic power of the (then) future president seemed at once premodern and a model of what modern authority should be. This was (as it happened) a time when major artists and intellectuals, black and white, both inside and outside the democratic movement, were beginning to rough out some ideas of what a post-apartheid culture might look like, in some cases either anticipating that culture in their own creative writing or seizing on its precocious appearance in that of others. The thrust of this case was that we needed a new literature of irony and the 'ordinary', freed from the polar conflict (the grand narrative, as it were) of oppressor and oppressed, and no longer fixated upon the pathos of injustice and its redress but dispersed instead across a range of differently oriented temporalities, positionalities and identities. My own contribution to this debate was then to suggest that the post-apartheid condition also needed non-coercive forms of authority, a purchase upon truth, sustaining myths, consensus: in short, if you like, its own post-traditional *wisdom*.[8] Not all irony is liberating, I argued, any more than all authority

---

[8] The best (in the sense that it is the most considered and scholarly) version of this argument for a post-apartheid culture is that presented by the South African writer and critic Njabulo Ndebele: see especially his 'Rediscovery of the Ordinary: Some New Writings in South Africa', in *South African Literature and Culture: Rediscovery of the Ordinary* (Manchester: Manchester University Press, 1994); my own 'contribution' to this debate is outlined in my 'Introduction' to Ndebele's book, and in the closing section of 'Not the Novel', and in Graham Pechey, 'Post-Apartheid Narratives', in *Colonial Discourse/Postcolonial Theory*, ed. by Francis Barker et al, (Manchester: Manchester University Press, 1994), pp. 151–71.

is oppressive. In this argument I drew on Bakhtin's later writings, with their modification of the earlier (almost exclusive) association of dialogism with the antagonistic modes of parody and polemic. I was especially drawn to their preoccupation with 'agreement', with the 'absolute responsive understanding' of the 'third' or 'superaddressee' who is implicitly posited in all exchanges, and among whose names are those of 'God' and 'posterity' (PT, 126–7). I was struck above all with the emphasis upon what he calls (in a pregnant, almost Gadamerian phrase) 'the mandatory nature of deep meaning' (PT, 121). These late-Bakhtinian concerns seemed to me peculiarly timely in a social text that was so radically recomposing itself as South Africa was (and still is), and where democratic consensus must at all costs not become as oppressive as the politics of institutionalised crisis which it replaced.

The post-apartheid condition that I am describing is of course a species of the genus postcolonial, one of the latest additions to the latter's phenomenal forms which does not simply passively join its fellows and leave the field where it was, but rather works to reconfigure the field itself. Meditating upon what 'post-apartheid' might mean has led me to reformulate the category of the postcolonial more decisively than ever away from any simple chronological or geographical or formal-political sense, and to speak of the postcolonial condition (at least in so far as it describes an order of being-in-the-world) as the phase one enters when one has seen not only that it takes anti-colonial struggles to produce neocolonial conditions, but that the neocolonial pathology draws its strength from the very pathos of anti-colonial assertion. Postcoloniality is the space beyond the deep collusion of imperialism and nationalism, those mirror-images of each other. The term cannot in this strong sense then be a description of any territory or constitutional arrangement or phase of history; of power secured and centrally exercised; or indeed of any kind of 'subject' or 'object'. In an Adornian expression, it is a moving 'forcefield' of possibilities and opportunities and difficulties which (as I have written elsewhere) 'carry within them the intimately cohabiting, mutually entailing negative and positive charges of both power and resistance' ('Post-Apartheid Narratives', 153). Postcoloniality is also that experiential paradox of a perennial imminence which will never fully arrive: it can be found haunting the corners of colonial and canonical texts and discourses of the past even as it acts as a countervailing force in the present to monopolistic political narratives and world orders both old and new, itself never becoming anything as grand or totalizing as an 'order'.

Perhaps above all else, though, the postcolonial is characterised by its promiscuous crossing and meeting of times: that is to say, by agendas and projects from any phase of history which had been marginalised by colonial forces about the business of domination, or by anticolonial forces no less busy with resistance. These might include gender battles, other forms of identity politics (including diasporic and 'anational' identities) that belong to late modernity. They might then also include (complicate and cross-fertilise) much earlier modes of spiritual self-assertion, in the form of those hybrid spiritualities so characteristic both of the African diaspora and of autochthonous Southern African communities, narratives of redemption which antedate the secular nationalism of mission-educated elites and in which the saints of Christianity and ancestors of precolonial belief unselfconsciously meet and mingle. These multifarious communities of believers with their dead or living prophets survive alongside the bigger battalions of the orthodox Christian denominations, and not without influence upon their liturgical culture. Postcolonial Christianity in Africa replays the faith's origins as a spiritual hybrid in the heteroglossia of the Mediterranean basin two millennia earlier.

Postcoloniality, in short, makes the universalism of the West look parochial and abstract, and it opens us to that dimension of 'great time' in which no meaning or value is ever absolutely lost. It might even suggest to us, against the reflexes of an earlier and aggressively historicizing and relativizing criticism of cultural texts, that the universals of humanism are not false-because-universal and therefore in dire need of having their noses rubbed in a (usually Marxist) meta-narrative of history, but rather not universal enough—in the sense of being not sufficiently welcoming of the boundlessness of meaning within which the finitude of our lives is played out. We might usefully bring all of this back to Bakhtin and help to connect the more familiar Bakhtinian themes with the rather later ones I have been privileging if we were to regard as 'postcolonial' any project of literature or language which takes its distance both from the metropolitan standard and from any nativist dogma of the purity of the vernacular, emphasising instead an ineluctable creolization which not only lies in the background of the standard itself (English being after all the most impure because historically the most pidginized of the Germanic languages), but also runs all the way from heard speech into the unheard depths of being and consciousness. That last clause is all-important: Bakhtin teaches us that hybridity of language has epistemological and ontological implications;

that it is not just an oddity exhausted by linguistic description or re-
ducible to its social causation.

The practice which makes this unheard creolization of consciousness
audible, which in so doing dialogizes the global heteroglossia of empire, is of course postcolonial writing.[9] It is about a hundred years
since the first native elites in the British Empire began answering back
to the centre: not in the early stages with a rival meta-narrative, but
rather by 'thinking with' the imperial narrative, 'innocently' re-
inflecting it towards emancipatory ends, opening up its aporias by its
own discursive means, holding the dominant discourse to its promises.
Transcendentalizing empire became in their hands not the legitimating
move it would be in the coloniser's; rather it is a gesture of disconcert-
ing mimicry by which the shortcomings of imperial practice on the
ground were thrown into relief. This moment of proto-nationalism in
which the official discourse of Empire was inwardly and seemingly
naively dialogized offers perhaps a richer yield of durable meanings
than the later, properly nationalist phase. The postcolonial condition
has more in common with the former than the latter, and loops back to
rejoin it. Nationalist writing answers imperialism's romance with realism, thereby remaining within the same economy of representation; silenced voices speak, becoming at one bound modern subjects. The
margin shows itself to be as good as the centre; the centre looks on
with pride.

Writing of the postcolonial condition, on the other hand (at once
centreless and multiply centred) compels imperial heteroglossia into a
polyphonic textuality, swallowing the flat earth of imperialism and
bringing it forth again as the sphere of a global community without
bounds, any point on which is a centre, any position an other for all the
others. The 'reverse colonisation' which has been a life experience for
millions of the colonised who have emigrated to the metropolis over
the last fifty years is only the literal realisation of a posture of migrancy
which underlies the best postcolonial writing of that period. Wherever
its producers are, whether they have stayed put in their place of birth
or moved on, such writing installs itself on the inside of the discourse
emitted by the erstwhile centre, reminding it of the breadth and reach

---

[9] The reader will notice that I have eschewed any illustrative examples of such writing: this has
been done partly because of the time constraints of the paper as it was delivered (which translate
into the space constraints of the present volume); partly because within such short compass any
such citation is a hostage to fortune, prompting questions of the kind 'What about *x* then?' I
leave it to readers to match the description I give of this writing against the work of their own
chosen candidates and to see if it fits.

of what its canonicity excludes. In the passage quoted in my epigraph Bakhtin astutely ascribes to the nineteenth century the miniaturisation and synchronisation of a universe of 'contextual meaning' which is infinite and omnitemporal. The age of European imperial expansion was an expansion of power only; where cultural texts were concerned, however, it was the reverse, a shrinking and atrophy of meaning. The centre's economic enrichment was in another respect its impoverishment; the modernisation that was elsewhere felt as epistemic violence closed rather than opened metropolitan horizons, in a travesty of the 'brave new world' of early modernity. The new writing of the old imperial periphery abolishes both centre and margins by equating them and by assuming the standpoint of a longer memory and a wider field of vision.

We are each of us a margin and each of us a centre: that way of putting it should ring bells for students of the early Bakhtin, who builds the whole house of value on the foundation of our 'outsideness' to one another, my authorship of you as 'hero' and your answering authorship of me (see AH). Writing in an imperial centre just shaken by revolution, Bakhtin along with other Russian-Orthodox intellectuals was seeking to fashion, from materials both traditional and modern, a Russian path to modernity that would avert the pathologies they had diagnosed in Western Europe's much earlier traversal of that route. Rather than rampantly modernizing in a rush to catch up (the route taken by those mainly socialist intellectuals leading its social transformation), Russia's 'world-historical' lateness with respect to the West was to be made into a virtue. A centre in the Asian context, Russia was globally speaking a cultural margin of Europe, and therefore well placed by its very 'outsideness' to re-author Europe's historical trajectory. That their project was a failure is no reason not to see the clear and suggestive analogy between Bakhtin and those versatile spiritual nomads, those exiles everywhere at home: the postcolonial writers of our time.

Rhythmic Cognition in the Reader:
Correcting Bakhtin's Wrong Turn

Donald Wesling

Mikhail Bakhtin must carry some responsibility for the effacement of poetry in the 1990s. Past International Bakhtin Conferences, in Manchester (1991), Mexico City (1993), and Moscow (1995) paid scant attention to poetry. Within the field of Bakhtin Studies, hardly anyone writing feminist dialogics or the dialogics of the oppressed is interested in an art so intricate, non-narrative, and deluxe. In the USA, over-professionalization (focus on writers not readers) is a factor, in creative writing programmes and specialized poetry magazines. Cultural Studies has added necessary perspectives, but except for rap lyrics, poetry stands for the genteel literary discipline this explosively emergent field is trying to overturn. Because the current definition of poetry (as less socially concerned and more monologic than the novel) inevitably influences whether and how we read, poetry's loss of importance is a direct result of how we theorize poetry. In Russia, after the Soviet era's glut of social concern, the situation of poetry is even more precarious, and many writers have stopped writing, in what is according to Mikhail Epstein 'perhaps the most radical of all existing variants of postmodernism', where

> *Glasnost* [...] takes to the greatest degree of perfection the post-modernist reduction of the world to a play of signifiers. [...] In the epoch of *glasnost*, there is perhaps one path remaining for true (*nastoiashchei*) literature: that of verbalized silence—or of the silenced word. To blurt out secrets so as not to divulge mysteries. [...] To preserve literature at the bottom of language, in its boundless silence. Such is the current poetics of the effacement of poetry.[1]

In this paper, I argue that Bakhtin's famous promotion of the dialogic novel at the expense of monologic poetry can be explained and, if we are generous, forgiven. That this effacement of poetry is not a fundamental error is proved by the many excellent studies that use the terms of Bakhtin's system, with rather than against Bakhtin, to interpret speech acts in poetry. The fundamental error is elsewhere: what he and his Circle and those working with his system have got wrong is the

---

[1] Mikhail Epstein, 'After the Future: On the New Consciousness in Literature', in *Late Soviet Culture: From Perestroika to Novostroika*, ed. by Thomas Lahusen with Gene Kuperman (Durham: Duke University Press, 1993), pp. 257–88 (p. 287).

meaning and role of *poetic rhythm*, which is what makes poetry poetry. The philosopher of great time has misunderstood the little time of
human acts of attention.

   A negative report designed to change the agenda should give the argument in its strongest form. However, to be fair to Bakhtin and critics
who use his terms, I should say that usually I find their dealings with
poetry admirable; I propose not critique but completion. Gary Saul
Morson and Caryl Emerson, in their magisterial but polemical *Creation of a Prosaics*, are right to insist that while Bakhtin is 'not immune
to [an] imperializing move on behalf of the novel', in the light of prosaics poetics may seem 'inadequate even for its own object, poetry';
once we 'examine prose in its own terms, we will come to see all verbal art, poetry included, in a different way'.[2] (At the end of this essay,
I shall argue that if this is true, it is strictly reversible: prosaics recruits
and corrects itself with ideas of rhythmic cognition invented in poetics.) Bakhtin, as Morson and Emerson admit, 'never did fully work
out' the implications of his approach for lyric poetry, and I agree, except that in my view given his premises he never could have worked
that out, and we inherit the task. It can be worked out only with premises generated, after Bakhtin's death, by theorists of rhythm like Henri
Meschonnic and Richard D. Cureton. The aim is to break through to a
rhythmics, and *thence* to a dialogics of lyric poetry, by finding and correcting Bakhtin's wrong turn.

   Bakhtin's own dealings with poetry and poetics are more extensive
than we would think from an encounter with his essay of 1934–1935,
'Discourse in the Novel', and even in that essay I see gestures towards
the end that partly modify the lyric-as-monologue claim of the opening;
and that essay has an amazing number of passing references to poems.
His poetry-friendly studies of sociological poetics, 'Discourse in Life
and Discourse in Poetry' (1926), and the *Formal Method in Literary
Scholarship* of 1928, were written while the enemy was still the detachable device rather than monologism. There he speaks of the inter-
relation of style and social meanings; he is wise about intonation, about
excessive theoreticism in stylistics and linguistics, about the mistake of
an exclusive focus on poetic devices, about the co-participant role of
the listener-reader. Bakhtin tends to admire epic and narrative poems,
where style and sound are de-emphasized, but he does give two long,
intelligent, early-twenties readings of the same personal lyric by Push-

---

[2] Gary Saul Morson and Caryl Emerson, *Mikhail Bakhtin: Creation of a Prosaics* (Stanford:
Stanford University Press, 1990), p. 20.

kin, 'Parting' ('Dlia beregov otchizny dal'noi'): eleven pages at the end of *Toward a Philosophy of the Act*, and twenty pages in the supplementary section of 'Author and Hero in Aesthetic Activity' (I will return to apply his categories from these Pushkin readings in my own description of Marina Tsvetaeva's 'Wires' (*Provoda*), a comparable poem on the theme of parting).

My search for recent English-language studies of poetry that use Bakhtin's terminology and ideas has yielded twenty-five articles and two books, and these I would divide into utterance-intonation studies like Don Bialostosky's book on Wordsworth, and heteroglossia studies with a political edge, like Robert Crawford's book on late twentieth-century world poetries in English.[3] Some of the articles, such as my own two on dialect poetry and on inner speech in recent UK writing, cross this line and take up both local speech acts and also the clashes of official and unofficial languages. Typical titles from the set of twenty-five are 'Reading Pound With Bakhtin: Sculpting the Social Languages of *Hugh Selwyn Mauberly*', or 'Marvell's Dialogics of History...', or 'John Clare's "Childe Harold": A Polyphonic Reading'. One of the most capacious of these articles is Lynn J. Shakinovsky's 'Hidden Listeners: Dialogism in the Poetry of Emily Dickinson'. Shakinovsky addresses the 'powerful powerlessness' of many of Dickinson's speakers, their 'efforts to gain monologic power, the illogicality of the texts, the split subject, and [...] the role of other suppressed voices in her poems'. Through close readings of three poems, she shows how boundaries are blurred between reader and addressee inside the text, how the reader is 'oddly implicated' even in the confusions—a poem's passive constructions, placement of dashes, or seemingly inept repetition of sounds. These are social aspects of the texts, and they display in language Dickinson's marginal existence as a woman and a poet. Briefly, with each of her examples, this critic refers to local effects of rhythm, but Shakinovsky is like all these articles and books, including my own, in largely avoiding the study of rhythmic phrasing. In over a thousand pages of Bakhtinian analysis, every one of

[3] Due to limited space, I give particulars only for the following: my own two Bakhtinian essays on poetry, 'Mikhail Bakhtin and the Social Poetics of Dialect', in *Papers on Language and Literature*, 29.3 (Summer 1993), 303–322, and '"Easier to Die Than to Remember": A Bakhtinian Reading of Basil Bunting', *Durham University Journal* (1995), 83–97; Lynn J. Shakinovsky, 'Hidden Listeners: Dialogism in the Poetry of Emily Dickinson', *Social Discourse/Discours Social*, 3.1–2 (Spring-Summer 1990), 199–214; Don H. Bialostosky, *Wordsworth, Dialogics and the Practice of Criticism* (Cambridge: Cambridge University Press, 1992); and Robert Crawford, *Identifying Poets: Self and Territory in Twentieth Century Poetry* (Edinburgh: Edinburgh University Press, 1993).

us has preferred to ask 'Who is Speaking?', rather than to ask about the multi-dimensional response-units of the reader; has preferred ideologeme-reading to skills-reading, intonation to rhythm, versification to cognition, metre to the encompassing category of rhythm. Is *that* the contribution of prosaics to poetics? *Prosaics*, the increasingly popular term for Bakhtin's theory of the novel and of communication acts generally, is a neologism formed on (and against) the term *Poetics*. To insist on the centrality of prosaics is to follow Bakhtin in relegating poetry and the theory of poetry; this allows us to map his thinking on aesthetics, speech-acts, and the novel. However, in our adhesion to his thought, our lack of dialogic distance, we are bound to repeat (or at least to miss seeing) his severe error, namely his inability to read poetry as an art of human expectation. Bakhtin flattens out and spatializes the theory of rhythm, and this, not his polemical praise of the novel, must be confronted first. Only then can we reconvert his prosaics back into a poetics of utterance, intonation, rhythmic phrasing, and history. In fact, Bakhtin is magnificent on the forms of meaning, but he is terribly conventional on the meanings of form; a full poetics will need to attend equally to, and to coordinate, both these modes of understanding. (Actually, Bakhtin does that successfully in the audio tape readings of German poems, which were heard by delegates to the Moscow Conference in June 1995. Bakhtin reads poetry aloud with great understanding and power, but that performance is not pertinent here; it is his theory of reading that is currently at issue.)

Much (fortunately not all) of my argument rests on my example and what I can do with it. My analysis of Marina Tsvetaeva's 'Wires' has less philosophical reach than Henri Meschonnic, less linguistic system than Richard Cureton; however, despite the limitations of one non-native surmise about rhythmic cognition in Russian, correcting Bakhtin's wrong turn will have *a priori* force if it can be done with reference to a powerful counter-theory. This is a case where having the better hypothesis is more important than providing a watertight, comprehensive analysis.

'Wires' is a diary poem in ten parts, written between mid-March and early April 1923, and published in *After Russia* (*Posle Rossii*). The poems are intellectual love-letters to Boris Pasternak, who was leaving Germany to return to the Russia forbidden to Tsvetaeva. Lily Feiler's 1994 biography describes Tsvetaeva's frantic agitation during the early twenties, when the exiled poet conducted several epistolary romances, projecting to distant, largely imaginary addressees the image of herself as erotic heroine; Catherine Ciepiela's 1996 *PMLA* article takes this perception down into the weave of metaphors of necessary absence in the poems: 'Tsvetaeva requires the absence of the beloved insofar as it involves the mediation of language'.[4] Tsvetaeva was wounding herself into creativity: the writing of her early exile is *cri de coeur* poetry, as pure an instance as one might find of what Bakhtin considers self-regarding lyric, largely sealed off from the community by the self-isolation of the speech-act and by the need to follow and derange a prescribed rhythmic pattern. If we could find elements of dialogism here, in such an extreme case, the discovery would help us to give equal privilege to poetry and prose; perhaps we could correct Bakhtin's wrong turn.

I propose to make two attempts at a reading of the opening poem in 'Wires'. In my first pass through Tsvetaeva's poem, I will try to account for it by the pertinent, indeed profound, but also limited analytical categories Bakhtin uses to read Pushkin's 'Parting', a poem of three eight-line stanzas. I believe these two congruent 1920s readings of the same poem are Bakhtin's only extensive readings of lyric. In my second attempt at reading Tsvetaeva, I will introduce a synthesis of terms and procedures more logically adequate from Iurii Tynianov, Meschonnic, and the American proponent of rhythmic phrasing, Cureton. I will show that the more logically adequate terms and procedures are also more practical, because they help us to account for more of Tsvetaeva's poem, and to read it as poetry and not, or as well as, something else.

In both of his studies, Bakhtin analyses Pushkin's 'Parting' as an end-of-essay example, in order to enforce points made in the body of his argument. His readings are presented not as afterthoughts but as confirmatory shifts down from exposition to an unusual (for him) depth of detail. In both essays he quotes the whole poem once in full, an

---

[4] Lily Feiler, *Marina Tsvetaeva: The Double Beat of Heaven and Hell* (Durham: Duke University Press, 1994), esp. pp. 140–41 for sentences on 'Wires' and Feiler's quotation of Tsvetaeva's tribute to Pasternak, 'brother in the fifth season and in the fourth dimension'; Catherine Ciepiela, 'The Demanding Woman Poet: On Resisting Marina Tsvetaeva,' *PMLA* 111. 3 (May 1996): 421–34 (p. 428). It will not be part of my assignment to show, against Bakhtin and Ciepiela, that poetry can be 'dialogical'; see Ciepiela's important article 'Taking Monologism Seriously: Bakhtin and Tsvetaeva's "The Pied Piper"', *Slavic Review* 53.4 (Winter 1994), 1010–24, in which she proposes that if we accept Bakhtin's description of poetry as monologic much in Tsvetaeva comes to light—hints of dialogue within the dominant monologue: 'To justify calling a poem "dialogical" in the Bakhtinian sense, one would first have to demonstrate the presence of ideological languages and then analyze the manner of their orchestration: are they monologically suppressed or dialogically allowed to speak their plural truths?' (p. 1014). Absolutely the right question.

admirable practice, and then quotes segments as he explains smaller units. In both essays he is as usual writing ethical and aesthetic theory in order to combat theoreticism. In both he follows his habit of checking the philosophical or literary act against speech-acts in the world. The term *architectonic* appears prominently in both readings, as Bakhtin's way of relating the two unique places of the speaker and his departed, now dead, Italian lover Riznich. 'The architectonic is something-*given* as well as something-*to-be-accomplished*, for it is the architectonic of an event' (TPA, 75). Here the *event* is physical distance as a foreshadowing of metaphysical separation. *Contraposition* shows the *outsideness* of lovers *vis-à-vis* one another, valuable because the only way we are defined is by others outside us in concrete moments of perception. *Outsideness* makes self-definition possible, as Pushkin shows in the authorial gesture that unifies remembered times and the *now*, and unifies the present-day grieving speaker-hero and the time after his own death when he will redeem Riznich's promise of a kiss: '*No zhdu ego: on za toboi*'. In *Toward a Philosophy of the Act*, whose analysis I have just given, Bakhtin says that the speaker and his lover are subordinated to Pushkin's authorial context, an author-preference he pushes harder in the 'Author and Hero' essay.

In 'Author and Hero' he refers to 'Parting' as 'this basically understandable poem', I suppose because he can find in it an opposition, which he pursues at length, between *intonation* and *formal intonation* in the lyric: 'the intonation of almost every word in the poem must be performed in three directions: the real-life intonation of the heroine, the equally real-life intonation of the hero, and the formal intonation of the author/reader', who integrates the different places, times, and points of view, from a stand-point external to them (AH, 212–13). In fact, the later 'Author and Hero' takes a less cautious view of these matters; while *Toward a Philosophy of the Act* ends its analysis and whole argument with the view that the I-Other contraposition produces 'an equivocation, a contradiction between form and content', 'Author and Hero' openly prefers real life to formal intention, and sets *intonation* against and above *rhythm*.

At one point earlier in 'Author and Hero' Bakhtin explicitly formulates the relationship of rhythm and intonation, those two processes that cannot be notated and that, as he says, must be 'surmised'. As Bakhtin says:

> The sound-image of a word is not only the bearer of rhythm, but is
> also thoroughly permeated by intonation, and in the actual reading
> of a work conflicts may arise between intonation and rhythm [...]
> rhythm represents, almost exclusively, a purely formal reaction of
> the *author* to the event as a *whole*, whereas intonation is [...] the
> intonational reaction of the *hero* to an object *within* the whole and
> [...] it is internally more differentiated and diversified. (AH, 215-16)

Here, in order to show 'the internal rhythm of the event', Bakhtin
actually uses a term from old-fashioned technical metrics: 'The *parting*
is the *arsis*, the promised meeting is the *thesis*; death is the *arsis*, yet
there will be a meeting, nevertheless—the *thesis*' (AH, 215). This is
unhelpful; I do not object to Bakhtin's account of the poem's multiple
times and persons, but rather to the way he takes rhythm as metre and
metre as a structural principle of alternation, extendable to huge non-
linguistic structures in the text. Here, on this page, Bakhtin needs to
see rhythm as a 'purely formal reaction of the author', separable from
thought and language and their reception by a reader. This resonates
with his disparagement of rhythm within the body of the 'Author and
Hero' essay, where he says the author as creator is free and active but
rhythm is unfree: 'My relationship to myself is incapable of being
rhythmical [...] in rhythm, as under narcosis, I am not conscious of myself' (AH, 120). From here, it is but a short step to the outright denun-
ciation of rhythm in 'Discourse in the Novel', a decade later:

> *Rhythm by creating an unmediated involvement between every as-*
> *pect of the accentual system of the whole* [...] destroys in embryo
> those social worlds of speech and of persons that are potentially
> embedded in the word [...] Rhythm serves to strengthen and con-
> centrate even further the unity and hermetic quality of the surface of
> poetic style, and of the unitary language that this style posits.
> (DN 298)

Everything that a refutation has to confront is in this passage: the emphasis on the author and the device, not on the reader's cognition; the
allegation that rhythm is solely individual and monologic, not social;
the sense that rhythm is a surface effect, and thus detachable. Usually
Bakhtin is more shaded and nuanced than that, yet the passage does
show his basic position.

Bakhtin might have analysed Tsvetaeva, because 'Wires' dates from
1923, almost exactly the moment of the two essays with pages on
Pushkin; of course, geopolitics and literary politics were against it. But

if he had done it, he might have described first the separation of the
speaker from her addressee and the slender link between them, that is
the telegraph wire. Here is the first of ten diary-dated poems in
'Wires':

> In a row of singing pillars,
> Supporting the Empyrean,
> I send to you my share
> Of the dale dust.
>   Along the alley
> Of sighs—with a wire to a pole—
> A telegraphic: I lo—o—ve...
>
> I plead...(a printed blank
> Won't fit it! It is simpler with wires!)
> These are pillars, on them Atlas
> Lowered a race track
> Of Olympian gods...
>   Along the pillars
> A telegraphic fa—are—well...
>
> Do you hear? This is the last breakdown
> Of a torn off throat: fa—are—well...
> These are riggings above a sea of fields,
> The quiet Atlantic path:
>
> Higher, higher—and we mer—ged
> In Ariadne's: re—turn,
>
> Turn around!...The melancholy
> Of charity hospitals: I won't get out!
> In the farewells of steel wires
> Are the voices of Hades
>
> Moving away... Conjuring
> The distance: pi—ty...
>
> Pity me! (In this chorus you will notice
> It?) In the death rattle
> Of obstinate passions is
> The breath of Eurydice:
>
> Through mounds and ditches
> Eurydice's: a—a—las,
>
> Don't lea—
>   *March 17*

Вереницею певчих свай,
Подпирающих Эмпиреи,
Посылаю тебе свой пай
Праха дольнего.
                        По аллее
Вздохов—проволокой к столбу—
Телеграфное: лю—ю—блю...

Умоляю... (печатный бланк
Не вместит! Проводами проще!)
Это—сваи, на них Атлант
Опустил скаковую площадь
Небожителей...
                        Вдоль свай
Телеграфное: про—о—щай...

Слышишь? Это последний срыв
Глотки сорванной: про—о—стите...
Это—снасти над морем нив,
Атлантический путь тихий:

Выше, выше—и сли—лись
В Ариаднино: ве—ер—нись,

Обернись!.. Даровых больниц
Заунывное: не выйду!
Это—проводами стальных
Проводов—голоса Аида

Удаляющиеся... Даль
Заклинающее: жа—аль...

Пожалейте! (В сем хоре—сей
Различаешь?) В предсмертном крике
Упирающихся страстей—
Дуновение Эвридики:

Через насыпи—и—рвы
Эвридикино: у—у—вы,

Не у—

                                    17 марта 1923[5]

---

[5] Marina Tsvetaeva, *After Russia/Posle Rossii*, trans. by Michael M. Naydan with Slava Yas-tremski, annotated by Michael M. Naydan (Ann Arbor: Ardis, 1992), pp. 96–99. Elaine Fein-stein's English free verse translation, which preserves the line of images but sacrifices metre, rhyme, stanza-structure, and punctuation, is not only a failure (all translations are failures), but a travesty. Eve Malleret's French versions of Tsvetaeva's even greater long poems of the same era, 'Poem of the Mountain' and 'Poem of the End', are far more satisfactory with similar short-line stanza poems of lost love. Malleret finds French substitutes for the original rhyme, metre, and

Bakhtin would have shown that the speaker is here in exile, and that
she implores her addressee not to return to Russia; this is a very different spatial-national issue from what occurs in the Pushkin poem. Exile
is a non-home for Tsvetaeva's hero, and she had hoped to make it into
an international art-home, with Pasternak nearby as co-equal crea-
tor/lover/listener/critic: to amplify this, Bakhtin would have quoted
Tsvetaeva's early-twenties prose letter to Pasternak, calling him
'brother in the fifth season and the fourth dimension' (see Feiler, note
6). He would have made something of the metaphor in the title:
'Wires' of the telegraph are fragile lines of contact, needing brevity
and prohibiting touch. Studying the poem's pattern of intonation,
Bakhtin might have shown how Russia, left behind by the speaker but
now Pasternak's object of desire, determines every feeling in the poem.
Tsvetaeva's best single book, which includes 'Wires', is entitled aggressively and despairingly *After Russia*, and Bakhtin could well define just those tones of voice, registering the violent self preoccupation of the speaker and the oddly naked dialogism of her private
verse-letter printed in a public book. Since he explicitly speaks in
praise of series-poems in the Pushkin passage in 'Author and Hero,'
Bakhtin would have appreciated the way a larger narrative is started
with this first letter-poem.

All to the good! Bakhtin would have seen a lot, though I suspect he
would be slightly shocked at the degree of lyric monologic intensity
here.

Remember now Bakhtin's typical and quietly dramatic statement in
his book on the Formal method, namely '*only* the *utterance* can be
beautiful'. In his wish to rehabilitate the primary speech genres, he can
do so only at the expense of secondary authorship. For him, monologism is an exaggeration of secondary, properly literary authorship, and
lyric poetry, which is in the first person and employs metrical rhythm,
is an exaggeration of monologism. Rhythm in this scheme is an abstraction from real experience and a restriction of freedom. But what if
we turn Bakhtin on his head, and with him virtually the entire tradition
of work on Russian and English prosody? What if we focus not on

---

punctuation: Marina Tsvétaéva, *Le Poème de la montagne/Le Poème de la fin*, trans. and pres.
by Eve Malleret (Lausanne: Editions L'Age d'Homme, 1984). Malleret's Tsvetaeva is Meschonnic's topic for the title essay of his *La Rime et la vie* (Paris: Editions Verdier, 1989), in which he
argues that Malleret uniquely catches the violence of sound in Tsvetaeva, a violence that is an
'oralization of language'; consequently, 'to freeverse [Tsvetaeva] is to break her principle of organization, her language, her rapport with the 19th century' (pp. 227, 219, my trans.).

versification—the text—but on verse rhythm—the reader? The alternative twentieth-century tradition I am sketching here begins with Tynianov's 1924 book *The Problem of Verse Language*, with his statement that once admitted into verse, *every* phonetic element becomes
'rhythmicized', and his demonstration that an artistic device involves a
relationship of 'complex interaction, not conjunction': in effect, a
struggle between rhythm and syntax, not their cooperation.[6]   Focused
on the device, Tynianov did not develop his intuition concerning how
the reader attends to larger discursive form. The next major step in my
story is Emile Benveniste's 1951 essay 'The Notion of Rhythm in its
Linguistic Expression'. I read Benveniste through his disciple
Meschonnic, who says that after Benveniste 'rhythm can no longer be
a sub-category of form. It is an organization (disposition, configura-
tion) of an *ensemble* [...] If rhythm is an organization of sense in a discourse it is no longer a distinct, juxtaposed level'.[7] Meschonnic devel-
ops Tynianov and Benveniste in *Critique du rythme*, where he argues
that 'If sense is an activity of the subject, if rhythm is an organisation
of sense in discourse, rhythm is necessarily an organisation or configu-
ration of the subject in his or her discourse' (*Critique du rythme*, 70–
71). Meschonnic does not perform many sample analyses in over seven
hundred pages; his task is not to develop a notation or to analyse poems, but to criticise a tradition of linguistic poetics and to propose a
new heading. His first aim is to use the subject-tied nature of rhythm to
refute Roman Jakobson's linguistics of the sign; but another explicit
aim (to which he devotes twenty pages) is to break down Bakhtin's
dualism of prose and poetry. Rhythm is an organisation of large and
small unities, inseparable from syntax, sense, and value in the poem;
whereas 'metrics', says Meschonnic, 'is the rhythm-theory of imbe-
ciles'. Individual, collective, new in each poem, rhythm is the orality of
a discourse; rhythm is the way the body gets into language and the way
the spoken gets into the written. Thus it is profoundly political.

   This story of an alternative tradition ends with Richard Cureton's
Rhythmic Phrasing in English Verse, a book which that takes its ori-

---

[6] Yuri Tynyanov, *The Problem of Verse Language*, trans. by M. Sousa and Brent Harvey (Ann
Arbor: Ardis, 1981), esp. p. 62.
[7] Emile Benveniste, 'La notion du "rythme" dans son expression linguistique', in *Problèmes de
linguistique générale* (Paris: Gallimard, 1966), pp. 327–35; I quote here from Meschonnic's
summary and comment in *Critique du rythme: anthropologie historique du langage* (Paris: Editions Verdier, 1982), pp. 69–73.

gins in cognitive psychology and music theory.[8] For Cureton, rhythmic
shape creates our experience of time in the poem: 'The simultaneous
arrays of projected beats, culminating groups and completing regions
that constitute rhythmic structure define shapes of cognitive and
physiological energy, shapes that, taken collectively and in concert, are
some of the most precise analogues of our emotional energies'
(Cureton, 426). As with Meschonnic, rhythm here is multidimensional,
top-down, and an effect of discourse. But Cureton goes far beyond
Meschonnic to validate intuitions about metre ('our rhythmic response
to regular pulsations in a perceptual medium'), grouping ('our rhythmic
response to points of structural culmination within delimited structural
spans'), and prolongation ('our rhythmic response [...] to anticipated
points of structural resolution/completion') (Cureton, 124–5). For him,
phrasal phenomena such as caesura and enjambement are more universal and expressively powerful than metrical forms.

Cureton takes his first one hundred and eighteen pages to describe
the severe limitations of current approaches and to refute the myths of
traditional prosody; he then takes another hundred and fifty-eight to
define rhythmic competence and his key variables of metre, grouping,
and prolongation, and to specify what he calls grouping well-
formedness rules, always demoting metre as the least powerful variable
in favour of mind-in-time, as we recognise patterns of anticipation, arrival, and recursive understanding of the whole poem. In his longest
chapter, 'Analysis', he then exhaustively analyses examples of free
verse, sprung rhythm, and pentameter; and he concludes with a short
chapter of only eighteen pages on implications for pedagogy and criticism. I have described the book's contents to show that Cureton per-
forms all the necessary logics of critique, affinity-finding, definition,
notation-proposing, and context building to deliver a complete theory.
The 'Analysis' chapter is crucial because there Cureton shows how a
single method can describe three poems which are extremely different
in structure. For example, his analysis of G. M. Hopkin's 'Windhover'
sonnet shows the poem syllable by syllable in a horizontal/vertical
tree-diagram; Cureton then reads the poem through eleven levels of

---

[8] Richard Cureton, *Rhythmic Phrasing in English Verse* (London and New York: Longman,
1992); I am more convinced by Richard Cureton's demonstration that weak-strong contrasts op-
erate at the lowest and mid-levels of phrasing, than I am by his contrasts at the highest levels,
i.e. above sentence and line. In my own, related book I argue that the most volatile and significant energy of thought is produced by the relationship of sentence and line, when these are coincident or non-coincident; *The Scissors of Meter: Grammetrics and Reading* (Ann Arbor: University of Michigan Press, 1996).

phrasing from the whole poem down to the syllable; then he shows centroidal groupings by deleting down from the highest levels; finally, he analyses line by metrical line to rebuild the reader's apprehension of the whole.

Cureton's back-and-forth is unwieldy but impressively complete in its re-imagining of the reader's thought processes. To demonstrate Cureton's method here would require that the protocols be performed for all ten poems of Tsvetaeva's 'Wires' series, showing the role of each poem within the series: plainly impossible because it would require hundreds of pages for grouping reductions and line by line analyses. Instead, I offer one person's reading of Tsvetaeva justified by Meschonnic's arguments and influenced by Cureton's definitions and method; an attempt to recapture, and turn into a narrative account, the experience of grouping, metre, and prolongation in the first poem in 'Wires', taking that poem as representative and offering perceptions on how it opens, and thus links itself to the rest of the series.

Let us return then to 'Wires'. If we consider rhythmic intent, which subsumes intonation, these are not just love letters to Pasternak, these are white-hot telegrams, abrupt, violent, jammed in phrasing for economy and frequently broken in transmission. Tsvetaeva's brevity is motivated by the idea of telegraphic concision. She can hardly utter a syllable, word, or phrase without throttling it, or imagining that telegraph technology has re-segmented her language, or diminished it within a 'chorus' ('voices', line 22; 'chorus', line 25) of other speakers who are crowding onto the same lines. 'Wires 1', unlike the other nine in the series, ends with a broken stanza, broken line, broken word: 'Don't lea—' must be completed by the reader as 'Don't leave'. The silent deleted syllables rouse a strong completion syndrome in the reader, leading on to the other nine telegrams-letters-cries-dated diary entries-death rattles, those Tsvetaevan speech genres of extremity, all of which do more than imply or apostrophize—they *grasp* and *bully* the addressee, who is Pasternak in the first instance but also, always, the reader amazed at the controlled violence of the utterance. This one moment at the end of the first poem, a jagged, premature closure that forces the reader's collaboration and thus intensifies and does not conclude the reader's mental energy, may lead us to the first of Cureton's categories of rhythmic hearing, what he calls grouping. This category pre-eminently requires harvesting the poem recursively, both ways from the centre, or backwards from the ending.

Grouping. We are discussing the rapport between a protagonist and her reader, and if we now move to reader-oriented strategies, the flow of conscious experience can be divided into large strong-weak oppositions across the poem as a whole. The reader registers through shifts of intonation and metaphor that Tsvetaeva begins with images of telegraph lines and of herself as hero, but she ends on a bald declaratory statement, having stripped off self-display. Other over-arching oppositions are part of grouping at the higher levels of intonation or metaphor: the height of telegraph wires against the sky versus the lowness of valley-dust (first two stanzas); 'singing pillars' of line 1 versus Hades of line 22 and the underworld 'mounds and ditches' of Eurydice at the end; the high clarity of a 'torn off throat' in the third (six-line) stanza versus subsumption in the chorus of the fifth; Eurydice (Tsvetaeva) versus Orpheus (Pasternak); the sending and questioning verbs of the first three stanzas versus the begging verbs of five and six ('Pity me!'; 'Don't lea—'); and within each stanza, the quatrain's narrative or vaunt versus the attached couplet's broken words and raw expression of need. More at the end than at the high detached opening, the speaker's language is crumbling and reverting to matter, under pressure of feeling. When the speaker flings down that broken word-line-stanza at the end (line 31 is a nascent, incomplete stanza), she leaves a garbled, incomplete message, and intonation units, already tiny in this poem, get even smaller toward the poem's final part-line.

Cureton finds centroidal patterns in the reader's temporal-semantic registration of the poem: my noticing of the relation of four-line to two-line segments within each stanza, the difference in rhetoric and intent, is just what he would claim is typical of a poet like Tsvetaeva, who divides even her smaller building blocks by further divisions. However, I see in Tsvetaeva another, far more unusual pattern, possibly unique to this poem and very much part of the rhetoric of its use of shortening intonation units in the line. One notes that hardly a single sentence is coincident with a line; it is sometimes even doubtful whether there *is* a sentence, whether there *is* a line. This instability is exaggerated by other devices: of the thirty-one lines, twenty are broken by typographical step-down, or by dashes, colons, suspension dots. There are mid-line and near-end-of-line breaks in lines already miniature, breaks within breaks and turns within turns. In fact, starting at the end of the first stanza, the poem tends to break in half *vertically, down the middle of each line.* The reader lurches from half-line to half-line, from line to line, word to word, syllable to syllable. This would be a strenuous enough rhetoric in cognition, but we must also register at the same time what is woven in semantically in changes of speech-act, allusions to literary and mythical figures, and in leaps from the grotesque to the sublime from one line to another (e.g., from charity hospitals to Hades). Tsvetaevan poetic grouping (as intonation, syntactic focus and thematic ornament) connives at maximum instability; Tsvetaevan time comes in a flurry of tiny units, which frequently change direction and manner of linkage before and behind.

Metre. When our concern is for rhythmic phrasing (for the architecture of the brain, and for the way humans pay attention to time within the verbal arts) metre loses its pre-eminence in versification; metre becomes one among several patterns of expectation to which we attend simultaneously. Rhythm cannot, although this is what Bakhtin seems to have argued, be reduced to metre. Rather, metre actualizes and reinforces rhythm. The binary and ternary metres in Tsvetaeva's short lines are combined in harsh and unexpected ways as part of the baffling of expectation produced. The intonation units are subdivided, and syntax is jammed or inverted in order to get rhymes on the same-number syllable in the line. Russian's avoidance of the forms of the verb 'to be', and the consequent replacement with 'eto' ('this/it/these/they [is/are]') in the middle-line of the three middle-stanzas in the poem, gives a rare beginning-of-line stress and sets up an unusual line that strives to right itself by the end of its short run. None of the 'eto' lines ends with one of the eight line-final pauses in the middles of words (e.g., line 6, 'liu—iu—bliu';'I lo—o—ve'). These words are highly unusual in producing hyperprosodic stresses: the dividing dashes call for additional stress, but when this happens, as Simon Karlinsky well says, Tsvetaeva 'violate[s] the very basis of Russian prosody by requiring more than one stress per word'.[9] If this happened once it would be an event with no implication for rhythmic phrasing; but it happens eight times at similar end-line position, creating a stutter-like refrain, a metrical effect that is part of the rhythmic punctuation of the poem, a sound effect that underscores the public nature of the telegram medium, its slippages away from the ideal of lyric intensity. When the poem is a telegram, the dash can be a metrical device and words can revert to their non-sense constituents. Thus across the grid of a fairly stable metrical structure and rhyme scheme (lines like wires) Tsvetaeva has written

---

[9] Simon Karlinsky, *Marina Cvetaeva: Her Life and Art* (Berkeley and Los Angeles: University of California Press, 1966), p. 162.

with punctuational excess, lexical instability,[10] and deliberate syntactic uncertainty. From the smallest particles of language, morphemes, through the volatile rank of the relation of line and sentence, up to the overall plot of failure to say farewell, this is 'The last breakdown / Of a torn off throat' (lines 13–14); this is a rhythm of rude wrenching.

Prolongation. While grouping and metre tend to be recursive, summative, over-arching, prolongation of the reader's attentional energies points forward: 'It divides the text into a hierarchy of prolongational *regions,* each of which is defined by a point of structural *arrival/departure*' (Cureton, 146). Hardly any of Tsvetaeva's lines and stanzas is stopped by syntax or full-period punctuation, so the poem's movement would seem headlong—except for the mid-line checks mentioned above; we get lurches from mid-line to mid-line, with quick turns at line-ends. Or we get words or part-words isolated as the line's last unstable syllable (lines 6, 12, 17, 18, 23, 24, 25, 29, 30, 31), an effect of toppling-over the ends of lines; but this particular prolongation is often stymied by an imperative the next line down: an 'arrival' at a new badgering verb (in one case playing on the Russian: *zh—al' / Pozhaleite*). The poem exaggerates transition by its stanza- and line-ends, and blocks transition by its line-starts and mid-line breaks, yielding stop-start stutter effects. Prolongational and metrical devices move in parallel with shortened intonational groupings, to saturate the reader's attentional energies. By these means, emblems of the force of her desire, the speaker attempts to eliminate the distance between herself and Pasternak, herself and the reader.

Tsvetaeva is Eurydice telling Orpheus not to go, but she is a poet also—and first. The ten sections of 'Wires' persistently raise the oppositions of Eurydice versus Orpheus, lips and arms versus writing, talking versus telegraphing. These are resolved, along with the paradox of distance between Tsvetaeva's exile-Hell and Pasternak's Russia, in the tenth poem's weird, daring assertion of a child born of Pasternak and the author, an illusionary creation that will rival natural birth. This is Tsvetaeva's final vaunt and hyperbole, sent out on telegraph wires to conquer them.

To come this far with the rhythms of 'Wires' is, I submit, to have done much to complete what was partial in Bakhtin's response to verse. To push this logic just one step further, however, we can say

---

[10] See the brilliant word-play on the instrumental plural *'próvodami'* ('In the farewells', line 21) and genitive plural *'provodóv'* ('of steel wires', line 22): the Russian words sound the same but are distinguished by stress (and the restriction of the former to the plural).

that Bakhtin has a tendency to state that poetry was the prestige form of an earlier era, and that the novel is the form of modernity. This is a history of genres that contributes to the effacement of poetry by prosaics. But what if we replay the logic of my argument in reverse? If Bakhtin (and most of his Circle, his followers, his students) can be so wrong about the reader's developing attention in the time of the poem, how can prosaics claim to *come after*? Prosaics has not theorized its own reading practice at the skills level, and lacks a terminology of grouping and prolongation with which to describe the movement of feeling in the novel. Perhaps one sour revenge of poetry and rhythmic phrasing will be to teach prosaics how to read, and to teach philosophers how to be critics and to know what we actually *do* when we read.

Women's Writing: an Ambivalent Politics

Pam Morris

One

Across a wide range of politically committed theoretical constituencies (gay and lesbian studies, Marxism, postcolonialism, gender and feminist studies) there is general agreement that the issue of identity constitutes an urgent conceptual challenge.[1] There is very little consensus, at present, on how that challenge might be resolved. The political imperative to retain categories of identity as locations of contestation vies with the need (equally political) to destabilise the coherence of any such defining term. Identity as a political rallying point is always ultimately an imaginary investment, and one that incurs the perils of factionalism and fanaticism. The aim of this paper is not to offer solutions to such complex and wide-reaching theoretical issues, but rather to address the more restricted question of how far women can speak, act and write from a political and ethical situatedness and yet avoid the fantasy of coherent identity. It is the nub of the problem, of course, that I must use the term 'women' to make my argument and in that sense cannot move outside the category I wish to put in question.

The issue of how far women can speak for themselves and how far they are spoken for or silenced by the language system has been answered in negative terms by (among others) Spivak, and, more recently, with cautious and judicious optimism by Judith Butler.[2] Within feminism generally, there has been a persistent attempt to theorize 'women's language' in some relation to the materiality of 'women's bodies'.[3] Initially, the female body tended to be perceived as an originating location of meaning beyond the determining confines of the symbolic order. This libidinal or biological essentialism has given way to recognition that bodies, as we know them, are produced in history: both generally as part of cultural production and as part of the psychic process that generates each subject.

---

[1] See, for example: Linda Alcoff, 'Cultural Feminism versus Poststructuralism: The Identity Crisis in Feminist Theory', *Signs*, 13 (1988), 405–36; and Chantal Mouffe, 'Feminism, Citizenship and Radical Democratic Politics', in *Feminists Theorize the Political*, ed. by Judith Butler and Joan W. Scott (London: Routledge, 1992), pp. 369–84.

[2] Gayatri Chakravorty Spivak, 'Can the Subaltern Speak?', in *Marxism and the Interpretation of Culture,* ed. by Cary Nelson and Lawrence Grossberg (Basingstoke: Macmillan, 1988), pp. 271–313; and Judith Butler, *Bodies That Matter* (London: Routledge, 1993).

[3] Within French feminism, the early work of Hélène Cixous and Luce Irigaray comes most obviously to mind, but American feminists Sandra Gilbert and Susan Gubar in their first work, *The Madwoman in the Attic* (New Haven: Yale University Press, 1979), also theorize women's writing in terms of bodily dis-ease.

This is the starting point of Butler's argument in *Bodies that Matter*, in which a notion of performativity is perceived as the reiterative practice of those 'regulatory norms' that produce and stabilise the embodied identity that they name, but equally and simultaneously make possible a citation of the norms that is not simple reiteration but insubordination (Butler, 45). Butler rereads the 'immutable' laws of the Lacanian symbolic as citational practices: 'a series of demands, taboos, sanctions, injunctions, prohibitions, [...] that wield the power to produce [...] sexual subjects' (Butler, 106). As this suggests, Butler's sense of citational practice is entirely concerned with orders of discourse. Although she refers to Freud's suggestion that 'bodily pain is the precondition of bodily self-discovery' (Butler, 58), she offers no account of those physical practices reiterated by and on bodies which produce female embodiment as 'natural'. Moreover, despite recasting the Lacanian symbolic as regulatory norms, Butler's thinking on these remains abstract and universalising, hence she cannot engage with either performativity or insubordination as specific events always situated in and determined by place and time.

I shall return to the problem of reiterative bodily practices towards the end of this paper. I want to begin by suggesting that Bakhtin's sense of language as event, rather than universal law, offers a more positive way forward here. In addition, in his writing on carnival, Bakhtin outlines a materialist and politicised perception of the body. The grotesque imagery of medieval popular culture affirms a profane celebration of bodily life and debases, decrowns, the abstract otherworldly idealism of religious ideology. Moreover, this is a perception of the body as produced in history. We might speculate that the process associated by Bakhtin with the eighteenth century whereby the grotesque, open, carnivalized representation of the body gives way to a closed, smoothed over, private body (RW, 320–23) has a particular bearing upon the increasing control exerted upon the female body during that period, and the confinement of women within the chaste enclosure of the domestic sphere. After this, women who remain in the public streets and squares are perceived only as degraded bodies for commercial exploitation. A complete abyss has opened up between the disembodied ideal of the angel in the house and the gross sensuality of the woman of the streets.

Bakhtin did not, of course, develop these potential insights in his work into the production and control of women's bodies. Indeed, feminists, among others, have pointed to the dubious nature of much of his writing on carnival. In particular, his ambivalent image of the female body as womb and tomb, as signified in the Kerch figurines of pregnant laughing hags—'pregnant death' as he terms it (RW, 25)— comes perilously close to stereotype. Celebratory representations of the womb as a naturalised principle of generation disguise the fact that begetting, pregnancy, birth and mothering are practices within geographical and historical worlds, and their experiential and reiterative meaning for women are wholly determined by those worlds. The cultural specificity of childbirth is one of the sharpest divisions fracturing the purely linguistic unity of 'women'. Class and race are pre-eminently the determinants of childbirth and death. Moreover, there is an asymmetry in cultural inscriptions of phallus and womb left unattended in Bakhtin's celebratory writing on the carnival body; too frequently in the real world the womb is merely the space in which phallic power constitutes itself. The carnival body, Bakhtin writes in *Rabelais and His World*, 'is the pregnant and begetting body, or at least a body ready for conception and fertilization' (RW, 26). It is impossible to read this undialogically, compartmentalised off from all the grotesque utilisation's of the 'ready' female body.

Bakhtin theorized carnival from his reading of texts by male authors, especially Dostoevskii. The work of women writers who make use of grotesque bodily imagery offers a positive way of re-theorizing the concept. However, before detailing this, I want to bring into focus two aspects of Bakhtin's earlier writing which have their basis in a firmly materialist sense of the body as occupying a specific time and space, and in language as an event performed within temporal and geographical parameters. These two aspects are: ethical practice as always a matter of embodied positioning, and discourse as ambivalent double-voicedness.

In 'Author and Hero in Aesthetic Activity', Bakhtin insists that the embodiment of a self has to be produced. It is not given naturally with birth and we cannot invent it for ourselves: 'The plastic value of my outer body has been as it were sculpted for me by the manifold acts of other people in relation to me' (AH, 49). It is only from outside the self that a sense of bodily and subject integrity can be gained. From within consciousness a sense of bodily identity can be experienced 'only in the form of scattered fragments, scraps, dangling on the string of my inner sensation of myself ' (AH, 28). It is only from a position outside the subject that closure and completion can be entertained. Contemplating another human being:

> parts of his body which are inaccessible to his own gaze (his head,
> his face and its expression), the world behind his back, and a whole
> series of objects and relations [...] are accessible to me but not to
> him. As we gaze at each other, two different worlds are reflected in
> the pupils of our eyes. [....] This ever-present *excess* of my seeing,
> knowing, and possessing in relation to any other human being is
> founded in the uniqueness and irreplaceability of my place in the
> world. For only I—the one-and-only I—occupy in a given set of
> circumstances this particular place at this particular time. (AH, 23)

This notion of an excess of seeing, deriving from what we may term
the absolute specificity of chronotopic embodiment, provides the basis
for a materialist ethics of 'answerability' or 'participative consciousness'. In *Toward a Philosophy of the Act*, Bakhtin argues that an ethical imperative cannot be defined by or derived from any constancy of
content or by any constant adherence to abstract principle, but must be
understood as a performative act of acknowledgement: 'It is not the
content of an obligation that obligates me, but my signature below it—
the fact that at one time I acknowledged or undersigned the given acknowledgement' (TPA, 38). This 'acknowledgement' is the product of
an actively participative understanding made possible by that excess of
seeing. This 'excess' entails a simultaneous inner and outer perception:
an act of empathetic identification with the other's inner consciousness
is brought into conjunction with an unrelinquished external perception
of the other. It is this moment of totalizing understanding, stemming
from 'the given once-occurrent point where I am now located, [and
where] no-one else has ever been located in the once-occurrent time
and once-occurrent space' that demands from me an answer, a compel-
lant obligation to 'say *this* word' (TPA, 40). The emphasis upon
uniqueness here is not intended to underwrite an individualistic perception of the subject, but, on the contrary, to make central to ethical
practice the notion of being positioned in relation to an other or others.
The obligation to perform *this* act, to speak *this* word is not placed
upon the subject by adherence to any abstract system of moral or political reasoning, but by answering the demands that arise from a
wholly specific subject position in time and space.

On the whole in Bakhtin's early essays, a relationship of love is emphasised between the subject who sees and the other who is encom-
passed in the excess of seeing. However, other possibilities are suggested if not developed. In *Toward a Philosophy of the Act*, Bakhtin
recognises that if understanding derives from the unique place of the
participative self in relation to any event, then there will be as many

valid ways of understanding that event as there are different subject positions possible within it. In that case 'perhaps we have to recognise doubt as constituting a quite distinctive sort of value?' (TPA, 45). The specific value of doubt, Bakhtin goes on to claim, is that it acts against the idea of truth as monolithic, as 'something determinate, finished, and petrified' (TPA, 45-46). It is this insight, which becomes central to Bakhtin's subsequent work, that affirms language as inherently double-voiced or dialogic. In this development the notion of excess of seeing becomes a sceptical relativism in which one view of the world, or one value system is brought into conjunction with another (an excess of seeing) so that the claims to monologic truth of either are put in doubt. This radical scepticism is materialised in those pervasive language forms that employ double-voicedness, especially parody, hidden polemic and hidden dialogue (the forms of which Bakhtin recognises and analyses most comprehensively in the writing of Dostoevskii). In such cases, Bakhtin says, 'we somehow detach ourselves from [our own words] [...] speak with an inner reservation [as] if we observe a certain distance from them, as if limiting our own authorship or dividing it in two' (PDP, 184).

This ambivalent or inner/outer relationship of the subject to their own discourse is further elaborated in the essay 'Discourse in the Novel', which suggests that the subject enters language by means of internalising the discourses of 'authoritative' and 'persuasive' others (DN, 342; 345). Ideological consciousness is initiated by an inner dialogism of these non-identical voices; this process is furthered as the subject discovers the decrowning power of double-voicedness. A sense of self is generated by a swing from love to ambivalence and scepticism as imitation of persuasive and authoritative others slides into parody. In such ambivalent discourse, Bakhtin suggests, it is possible to translate 'one's own intentions from one linguistic system to another [...] [to say] "I am me" in someone else's language, and in my own language, "I am other"' (DN, 315). It is this ability of the subject to occupy a double position within sign systems that makes possible the ability to doubt any absolute bonding of ideological meaning to a signifying practice.

Bakhtin's writing provides the foundation for the work of Julia Kristeva, who, in an essay on Bakhtin, underlines the importance of the internalisation of contending social voices for the possibility of an interventionist writing. It is this sense of language as dialogic that allows a writer to 'enter history' as a participative consciousness rather than remaining enclosed within ideology. This relativizing of one sign system against another, she writes, produces an 'ambivalent ethics: negation as affirmation', since an impulse of decrowning or debasement of authoritative Truth inevitably affirms truth in and by that act of nega-tion.[4] In *Revolution in Poetic Language,* Kristeva uses the term *inter-textuality* to denote 'transposition of one (or several) sign system(s) into another', an operation which undermines doxy and brings about 'the destruction of the old position and the formation of a new one'.[5]

Kristeva provides a more rigorous theoretical underpinning for Bakhtin's notions of ambivalence and embodiment by elaborating them in terms of the psychoanalytic concepts of introjection and expulsion. It is by means of the physical processes of ingestion and expulsion that the subject materialises its self as embodied. Kristeva describes this process in strikingly Rabelaisian imagery:

> Since food is not an 'other' for me [...] I expel *myself,* I spit *myself* out, I abject *myself* within the same motion through which 'I' claim to establish myself [...] guts sprawling [...] I give birth to myself amid the violence of sobs, of vomit [...] These body fluids, this de-filement, this shit are what life withstands [...] There, I am at the border of my condition as a living being. My body extricates itself, as being alive, from that border.[6]

The most intensely charged boundary from which the unformed subject must extricate a self is that with the lovingly introjected maternal body. The mouth which spits out the mother strives simultaneously to recap-ture that loss in words: 'Through the mouth that I fill with words in-stead of my mother whom I miss from now on more than ever, I elabo-rate that want, and the aggressivity that accompanies it, by *saying*' (*Powers of Horror,* 4). Thus language and the subject are constituted in and by ambivalence, and it is this initiating impulse of insubordina-tion in discourse that any monologic order has to work continually to suppress. The mother is the beloved object of the first mimetic, narcis-sistic self-imaging, but this is a loving gift of identity that is always sliding through ambivalence into scepticism and parody. The child's 'no' is simultaneously an internalisation of the maternal voice and a mocking 'citation as insubordination'—to use Judith Butler's phrase. Kristeva writes of a consciousness of the self as 'fake', which arises

---

[4] Julia Kristeva, 'Word, Dialogue and Novel', in *Desire in Language: A Semiotic Approach to Literature and Art,* ed. by Leon S. Roudiez, trans. by Thomas Gora, Alice Jardine and Leon S. Roudiez (Oxford: Blackwell, 1981), pp. 64–91 (p. 69).

[5] *Revolution in Poetic Language,* trans. by Margaret Waller (New York: Columbia University Press, 1984), pp. 59–60.

[6] Julia Kristeva, *Powers of Horror: An Essay on Abjection,* trans. by Leon S. Roudiez (New York: Columbia University Press, 1982), p. 3.

'because one rarely succeeds in identifying fully with an ideal' and this faking 'challenges the universe of established values, pokes fun at them'.[7]

All speaking subjects, male and female, must retain this potential to constitute themselves discursively from one sign system into another, to say 'I am me' in someone else's language, and in my own language, 'I am other'. However, an argument can be made that female subjects have privileged access to this ambivalent subject positioning; in other words that they more frequently tend to be both spectators and participants within their own discursive performances. Following Freud, Kristeva suggests that the female child's experience of the process of abjection is both more complicated than a male child's and less final and extreme.[8] The introjected maternal body is never wholly expelled and, in addition, there is a specular identification with the mother. This internal and external identification constitutes an excess of seeing that produces a subject doubly positioned; a consciousness split between scepticism towards and performance of a normative gender role—the ideal that we never quite identify with. For this reason, women are more readily aware of the performative quality—the faking—of a feminine identity. And this would explain why women's writing seems so frequently to construct a double consciousness whereby a spectating 'I' seems to watch a social identity perform as a 'woman' with comic, knowing scepticism—a quality Kristeva refers to as women's ironic common sense.

However, this comic excess of seeing is genuinely ambivalent. While it ironises the 'Truth' of all idealising discourses of the maternal and the feminine, it does not finally or totally reject such an identification. It constructs what we may call a sceptical commitment that refuses to take the truth of womanly identity seriously yet preserves an intuition of maternal love as a glimpsed basis of utopian practice. It is this quality of sceptical commitment that I want to associate with some writing by women. However, before turning to that, the legitimate criticism brought against psychoanalytic theory for the unacknowledged and unquestioned universalism of its founding assumptions has to be met. Kristeva's essay 'Women's Time' suggests that we might situate women simultaneously within two conceptions of temporality: linear

---

[7] Julia Kristeva, *Tales of Love*, trans. by Leon S. Roudiez (New York: Columbia University Press, 1987), pp. 126–27.
[8] Julia Kristeva, *Black Sun: Depression and Melancholia*, trans. by Leon S. Roudiez (New York: Columbia University Press, 1989), pp. 28–29.

and cyclical time.[9] Women across different cultures and histories are
unified through their structural position within the reproductive cycle,
but that structural position derives its meaning and its experienced
form from the determinants of linear time; from the social specificity
that alone constitutes each historical moment. In this way, women may
be thought of as sharing the potential for an ambivalent ethics due to
their place within the reproductive structure, but the articulation of that
ethics will be entirely shaped by the specifics of their chronotopic embodiment.

Two

Angela Carter has acknowledged that her own recognition of feminine
identity as a fake derives from a very specific situation within European linear history:

> I can date to that [...] sense of heightened awareness [...] in the
> summer of 1968 my own questioning of the nature of my reality as
> a *woman*. How that social fiction of my 'femininity' was created, by
> means outside my control, and palmed off on me as the real thing.[10]

The term carnival is regularly invoked in discussions of Carter's work,
but often in an unspecified, certainly uninterrogated way.[11] However,
recognising that a carnivalesque consciousness provides the generative
principle within all her writing helps to bring into focus its political
agenda and the ambitious revisioning of carnival imagery and structures that she achieves.

The defining vitality of Carter's mature fiction is its extraordinary
movement through whole constellations of sign systems. In *Nights at
the Circus,* she constructs a brilliant modern version of the mennipea,
combining in it every quality noted by Bakhtin: a carnivalesque form of
comedy; a bold and unrestrained use of fantasy and extraordinary
situations for provoking and testing philosophical ideas relating to
'ultimate questions' of human existence; slum naturalism; experimental
fantasticality, often to allow for the representation of abnormal and ex-

[9] Julia Kristeva, 'Women's Time' in *The Kristeva Reader*, ed. by Toril Moi (Oxford: Blackwell, 1986), pp. 187–213 (pp. 189–90).
[10] *On Gender and Writing*, ed. by Michelene Wander (London: Pandora Press, 1983), p. 70.
[11] Sally Robinson, in *Engendering the Subject: Gender and Self-Representation in Contempo-rary Women's Fiction* (Albany: State University of New York, 1991), does offer a detailed ac-count of Carter's use of parody and doubled narrative consciousness, but she draws upon the work of Irigaray and Derrida, rather than Bakhtin.

treme moral and psychic states; emphasis on scandal scenes, eccentricity and breaches of decorum; elements of social utopia and of current and topical issues; and, finally, the insertion of many genres to produce a multi-voiced dialogic text (PDP, 114–18). In fact, *Nights at the Circus* is a cacophony of parodic discourses from almost every generic tradition feeding into the novel, including fairy tales, nineteenth-century realism, detective fiction, journalism, travel writing and popular romance. Earlier texts, like *The Bloody Chamber,* are produced from revisionary combinations of cultural myths and legends, gothic fiction and Blakean themes. *Wise Children* represents a carnivalesque assault upon the whole tradition and canon of Shakespeare, focusing specially upon Shakespeare's own most carnivalesque play: *A Midsummer's Night Dream.* However, this 'novelizing' of past, usually male, literary authorities is genuinely carnivalesque in Bakhtin's sense of the word. Carter's parody of generic forms and great traditions is always ambivalent. Her rewritings stem from an affirmative impulse of love for, as well as hostility to, the respected literary forms she mockingly appropriates; it is the process of negation as affirmation that she undertakes.

As well as parodic transposition of sign systems, Carter's writing persistently thematises an impulse of abasement; an emphasis upon the body as open, excreting and messily physical. Like Rabelais, she is attracted to the way fairs and market places make public this physicality as spectacle:

> There's a lack of reticence about the displays [...] It grabs you at the visceral level. Meat lies on the slab in moist bleeding chunks everything, tongue, liver, kidneys, terribly recognisable as such. [...] The girl at the cheese stall brusquely offers you a sliver of Cheddar on the end of a murderous knife [...] The rituals of buying and selling involve a direct face to face confrontation. [...] These enormous markets of the great northern cities are like the peasant markets of Europe or even like oriental bazaars.[12]

As in Rabelais's writing, Carter here fuses life and death into unified images: the offer of food on a murderous knife.

In her fiction the impulses of abasement and confrontation are used strategically to bring into question the nature of the divisive and containing identity boundaries of gender, class and nation. Heroines, in her stories, are invariably removed from a clean, safe, private, bourgeois

---

[12] Angela Carter, *Nothing Sacred: Selected Writings* (London: Virago, 1982), pp. 67–69.

domestic world and forced into a more public space, unprotected from face to face confrontations with a sensuous, procreative, but smelly bodily proximity. Despite, however, using grotesque realism to insist upon the physicality of bodily life, Carter offers no celebratory images of the procreative womb. Indeed, she is highly sceptical of all idealising myths of the feminine, and in her non-fictional work, *The Sadeian Women,* she undertakes a rigorous demolition of cultural mystifications of women's identity. Women, she says, should reject 'the bankrupt enchantments of the womb' as one of the 'most damaging of all consolatory fictions', since it puts any woman who subscribes to it into 'voluntary exile from the historical world'; she insists that 'mother goddesses are just as silly a notion as father gods'.[13]

It is this impulse to decrown mythic mothers that produces Carter's distinctively feminist reworking of carnival imagery. In her early fiction especially, there is a strong movement of negation against the maternal; mothers are either dead or absent from most stories. She has said that houses, particularly empty ones, symbolise the maternal for her.[14] They feature in her work as ruined, abandoned, falling to pieces, and often they are exploded or consumed in flames as in the carnival bonfire that concludes *The Magic Toyshop.* The destructive impulse against the maternal ideal reaches its comic climax in *The Passion of the New Eve* with its grossly parodic castrating Mother. As a brilliant surgeon, Mother makes use of science-fiction technology to sculpt her gargantuan flesh into a grotesque celebration of maternity, including two rows of massive breasts. Mother, enclosed deep in subterranean caves, is a self-made monstrous mythological artefact; a vengeful carnival figure produced from all the cultural fantasies, dreams and nightmares located in the maternal.

Carter's two final novels, *Nights at the Circus* and *Wise Children,* make use of grotesque bodily realism to carnivalize cultural idealisations of feminine sexual glamour, those figurings of the female body as smoothed over, glossy, eternally youthful, and without the slightest taint of the actually physical. By contrast, Fevvers, the heroine of *Nights at the Circus,* is a gargantuan figure with an appetite to match. In keeping with the mennipean form of the novel, she is represented as scandalously breaching the norms of feminine decorum, feasting gluttonously on eel pie, belching loudly with satisfaction, peeing openly in

---

[13] Angela Carter, *The Sadeian Woman: An Exercise in Cultural History* (London: Virago, 1979), pp. 109; 105.
[14] 'Interview with Lorna Sage' in *New Writing,* ed. by Malcolm Bradbury and Judy Cooke (London: Minerva Press, 1992), p. 190.

her dressing-room, while swigging quantities of champagne; a profane celebration of the open, ingesting, and excreting body. Nevertheless, despite the heightened emphasis upon earthy materiality, Fevvers is an ambivalent figure; the downward movement of bodily abasement is counteracted by an upward impulse of aspiration. She defies the power of gravity and the womb; she spreads wings and flies. There is nothing ethereal about this, however; the prose emphasises the grotesque bodily weight of her slow, ungainly upward flight in a way which pokes fun at all those pious myths of the feminine as a spiritualised, disembodied ideal. Fevvers is distinctly not the angel in the house. Carter constructs a fully ambivalent carnival figure, mocking both normative and idealising accounts of the feminine and affirming a new figuring which unites embodiment and aspiration, a down-to-earth materiality with the freedom for remaking. This representation also mocks Bakhtin's version of the downward carnival movement which so often functions in his writing to ensovereign a universal womb. In Fevvers the bulge of female belly has shifted upwards to become the hump of wings for flight. Moreover, this hump brings about another reversal of hierarchy; Fevvers' wings ensure that she cannot be placed in the missionary position. Fevvers must always fuck on top.

In *Wise Children,* the heroines, Nora and Dora, carnival doubles of laughing but definitely unpregnant hags, paint youthful beauty in makeup several inches thick onto their aged faces. These masks dissolve the boundaries between youth and age, beauty and the grotesque, birth and death, and male and female. 'It took us an age, but we did it; we painted the faces that we always used to have on to the faces we have now. [...] "It's every woman's tragedy", said Nora, as we contemplated our masterpieces, "that, after a certain age, she looks like a female impersonator".'[15] As this suggests, Nora and Dora, as professional performers, are fully alive to the parodic potential of becoming sceptical spectators of the self as social identity. Indeed, for twins that spectator-participant excess of seeing is staged in embodied form.

In an interview given just after she had written *Wise Children,* Carter suggested that women, unlike men, are forced into awareness that identity is not natural, that it is a fiction and invention (*New Writing,* 189). This perception is perhaps the reason for the swing to an affirmation of performance and masking in her last works as opposed to the earlier negative representation of masks as imposed and confining social norms. By becoming a clown, the hero of *Nights at the Circus*

---

[15] Angela Carter, *Wise Children* (London: Vintage, 1991), p. 192.

experiences 'a vertiginous sense of freedom [...] the freedom that lies behind the mask, within dissimulation, the freedom to juggle with being, and indeed with language which is vital with our being, that lies at the heart of burlesque'.[16] However, it is the heroine who is represented as most consciously grasping the potential language offers for juggling with being. It is her narrative that most fully utilises the ability to say 'I am me' in some one else's language, and in my own language 'I am other'. Fevvers constructs a biography out of an absurd intertextuality of discourses, thereby pointing to the parodic fiction of all identity. At the beginning of her story, Fevvers 'confronts herself with a grin in the mirror as she ripped six inches of fake lash from her left eyelid' (*Nights at the Circus*, 7). That complicitous grin at the imaged self acknowledges, underwrites, with a comic yet affirming scepticism, an identity she has committed herself to perform.

However, for actors the commitment to perform is a wholly serious obligation while the contract runs. It is perhaps for this reason that actors and theatrical troopers predominate in the last novels. For in these texts, finally, there is an affirming commitment to that most confining of social roles: mothering. In these novels, motherhood is rigorously disconnected from biology and the womb. Mothers make themselves, not by any surgical sculpting of flesh, but by 'answering' the demands arising out of very specific situations of need. 'Mother is as mother does', a character says in *Wise Children* (223). The vast heroine, Fevvers, who 'never docked via what you might call *normal channels*' (*Nights at the Circus*, 7), is lovingly fostered by the diminutive Lizzie, who teaches herself, by watching nesting birds, how to perform the role of mother bird in answer to Fevvers' need to fly. Nora and Dora push home the pram containing orphaned twins they have impulsively adopted, singing, 'We can't give you anything but love, babies' (*Wise Children*, 231). Significantly, the song belongs to music hall and the pram is pushed through the streets; there is no retreat in this mothering from public space into domestic privacy or into idealised myth. The obligation accepted is to a practice, not an identity, a wry, yet utopian commitment to perform in answer to the understood needs of another. And the need of the other is self-empowerment: to learn to fly.

Carter's utopianism derives perhaps from that shaping moment of consciousness for her as a writer in the late 1960s. Her recuperation of the maternal as social answerability offers a productive metaphor for rethinking categories of political identity. The carnivalesque attack

---

[16] Angela Carter, *Nights at the Circus* (London: Pan Books, 1985), p. 103.

upon the maternal as oppressive myth swings back to an affirmative refiguring of mothering as a trope for a practice of commitment. However, it has to be said that Carter's optimism is maintained by a necessary disavowal of temporality; her narratives unfold in ahistorical dreamtime and so do not track those repetitive practices that produce identity as naturalised submission to fate.

Three

The work of Mahasweta Devi is produced in 'answer' to the bleak demands of late capitalist, post-colonial India. Not surprisingly, her writing seems to have few points of contact with that of Carter. However, the defining quality of Devi's fictional language is intense dialogic contestation. Single sentences move through whole sequences of different sign systems so that ironising doubt is the generating principle of structure. Her stories are almost wholly constituted of voices; a dense intertextuality of social discourses. Every voice, even the most fragmentary, articulates an ideological view of the world so that what is materialised in words are jostling confrontations of multiple, often contradictory cultural perspectives: classes, castes, generations, religion, westernised thinking and traditional belief, men and women, educated and unschooled. Devi's narratives unfold in public space, and for the lowest class of impoverished characters in her fiction there exists no safe private zone. Bodies are casually broken in the streets as cars drive unnoticingly over the legs of those who walk. 'Decolonization has not reached the poor,' Devi says, 'that is why these things happen. Women are just merchandise, commodities'.[17]

In Devi's stories the representation of the female body, as breasts, womb and genitals, is precisely located as the material site of multiple forms of exploitation, degradation, bonded labour and enforced production. Her heroines are shown as situated at the intersection of the forces of nationalism, world capitalism and residual traditionalism, a complex economic and ideological nexus that produces a 'ready' female body whose 'self' is excluded from control of its productive forces and their surplus value. Devi makes use of grotesque bodily imagery to juxtapose this commodification of women to the mystifying idealisation of maternity employed alike by traditional religious discourse and by the new nationalist rhetoric of 'Mother India', as interpellative strategy constituting the imaginary unity of the nation.

---

[17] Mahasweta Devi, *Imaginary Maps*, trans. by Gayatri Chakravorty Spivak (London: Routledge, 1995), p. xx.

The narrative impetus of the stories is provided by the impelling power of these social discourses upon the lives of the characters, but these networks of words are always attached to economic networks. In 'Douloti the Bountiful', bonded agricultural labourers are subjected to a combination of the persuasive discourse of liberal national politics with the authoritative language of religion to procure their daughters as prostitutes in the regional towns. Douloti's father is approached by a brahman offering to purchase his freedom from bonded labour in return for 'marriage' to his daughter: 'In the present age the brahman is the liberator of the untouchable' (*Imaginary Maps*, 46).

In the story 'Breast-Giver' the determinants of the plot arise from a similarly specific moment of interchange between traditional sanctities and late twentieth-century global capitalism. The heroine, named Jashoda after the divine mother, wife of Krishna, is employed by the wealthy Haldar family as wet-nurse to their many children. The family's money was made from profiteering during the war as allies to the British, and within that older generation a westernised materialism co-exists complacently with a sentimentalised religious reverence. However, the demand for Jashoda's milk comes from the younger post-war generation of Haldar wives. For them, the idealised image of femininity is not the divine Jashoda, pregnant mother of the world, but westernised, consumer-orientated sexual glamour. This desire conflicts directly with the traditional demands of submissive maternity. In the story, the Haldar women solve their modern problem by exploiting the impoverished Jashoda's adherence to the traditional myth of maternal divinity. She is paid food to suckle their successive offspring so that they 'can keep their figures. They can wear blouses and bras of "European cut"'.[18]

By contrast, the persuasive and authoritative discourse of divinely blessed and natural motherhood is represented as producing Jashoda's complicity in her own exploitation. Interpellated as 'holy mother', Jashoda 'willingly' conscripts her body to perform the functions of her only perceived self. Constant pregnancy to ensure the continued supply of milk is a reiterative practice that produces an identity of mother as natural. Jashoda's character discourse is used to trace the process of alienation whereby her own body becomes merely a means of economic livelihood. It is the 'job' of her breasts to hold milk: 'I'm going to pull our weight with these', she boasts (*Other Worlds*, 228). The intersection of such westernised, economic terminology with religious

---

[18] Mahasweta Devi, 'Breast-Giver', in *Other Worlds: Essays in Cultural Politics*, trans. by Gayatri Chakravorty Spivak (London: Routledge, 1988), p. 229.

discourse foregrounds the doubly alienated relation of Jashoda to her own body as productive force. Total self loss is recast in the hyperbolic rhetoric of the divine and ceaseless blessing of procreativity. In this way fictional discourse materialises a bitter parody of the spectator-participant splitting of self. Jashoda is the proud, not the sceptical, spectator of her body's over-brimming lactation, and unconscious of the economic exploitation she lives. Jashoda is proud that she is 'by *profession* a mother' (*Other Worlds*, 228). The italicised word, suggestive of westernised individualist feminist claims for the right to independent livelihood, pinpoints a bitter irony. It is the desire of the wealthy Haldar women to embrace western values that has determined Jashoda's employment. Jashoda 'professes' an identity as mother, but she can attain no vantage point in discourse, no excess of seeing, to question its truth; her sense of self is bonded to a physically inscribed norm: 'she never had time to calculate if she could or could not bear motherhood. Motherhood was always her way of living' (*Other Worlds*, 222).

An even more brutal process of bodily alienation is represented in 'Douloti the Bountiful'. The dark underside of Indian religious veneration of female procreativity is a belief that male virility is strengthened by intercourse with a virgin. Thus mystification of female flesh inflates the market price of young girls. Religious mythology intersects with economic power so that the owners of bonded labour can increase their profits by facilitating (for a payment) the procurement of the wives and daughters of the labourers bonded to their land. This is the fate of the heroine Douloti and again the female body as produced by a brutal reiterative practice of enforced sexual slavery is experienced as the alienated location of a conscripted natural identity: 'The boss has made them land. He plows and plows their bodies' land and raises a crop [...] Why should Douloti be afraid? She has understood now that this is natural. Now she has no fear, no sorrow, no desire' (*Imaginary Maps*, 160–1). Traditional respect for hierarchy preserves favoured prostitutes, like Douloti, as sole possessions of the more important clients so that a degree of paternalism can co-exist within the brutality of the sexual transaction. Soon, however, the influence of western commodification and maximisation of profit dictates that it makes better business sense to utilise the women's bodies continuously even if at a lower price per client.

Devi makes use of grotesque bodily imagery to foreground the brutalised reality of women as commodities, counterpoising the open, stinking, and excreting female body to the sanctified rhetorics which collaborate in the processes of its exploitation and degradation. At the end of 'Breast-Giver' Jashoda's breasts, previously identified with the Holy Cow, Mother of the World, ulcerate into stinking cancerous wounds which keep mocking her 'with a hundred mouths' (*Other Worlds*, 236). Her left breast 'bursts like the crater of a volcano' and 'the smell of putrefaction makes approach difficult' (240). Physical disgust, pain, isolation are foregrounded in contrast to the sentimental religious mythology that interpellated Jashoda as mother. In 'Douloti the Bountiful', the traditional veneration of the Holy Mother is shown as transposed into a new signifying system of national identity. The bonded labourers are complacently assured that as children of the same mother, Mother India, 'you are all independent India's free people' (*Imaginary Maps*, 41). Douloti's sexual enslavement is the reality underlying that consolatory myth of imaginary interpellation of people as nation. At the end of the story, her 'tormented corpse, putrified with venereal disease, having vomited up all the blood in its desiccated lungs' becomes a public spectacle lying across a map of India, drawn in the dust in celebration of Independence Day (93).

These bitterly parodic refigurings in Devi's writing of the religious, national, and naturalising myths of the feminine body, stage a violent negation of those various cultural forms of metaphoric abstraction that disembody the female subject. What is insisted upon is the open, vulnerable materiality of women as bodies. For that reason the figuring of Douloti and Jashoda should not be read as metaphoric substitutions for an India corrupted by greed and western materialism. On the contrary, Devi uses grotesque bodily imagery in the reverse way, to re-identify the nation with its many specific embodied female subjects, situated at precise conjunctions of national history. The mystifying totality of the nation, as mother of all its people, is fractured and abased by the embodiment, open, defiled, excreting, of Douloti as specific subject, subjected to the historical and cultural contradictions inherent in the nation as many.

Carter makes revisionary use of carnival discourse to decrown idealising and naturalising female identities, but in her last two novels a positive sense of performativity allows her to refigure the maternal as an ambivalent politics. Answering the needs of another calls forth practice as a serious yet ironised commitment. Devi likewise uses grotesque bodily imagery to savage myths of feminine identity, but her main female characters are represented as alienated naturalised bodies, produced by reiterative physical practices, and as wholly enclosed within mystifying discourses. An ambivalent commitment is not located in the heroines but in the polyphonic practice of the prose style. The narratives are structured almost entirely as dialogue, even those passages not written as direct speech are intonated as specific points of view. The narrator's voice, where distinguishable as such, assumes no authority or omniscience, but speaks from the same discursive level as that of a character. Unlike the characters, though, the narrator is not enclosed within a unitary perspective. The narrative voice is profoundly ventriloquist, its ideological scepticism materialised in a pervasive ironic relativizing of one discourse against another. However, what this constructs, as an alternative to linguistic enclosure, is not a postmodern fragmentation of any and all subject positions, but a very specifically situated hidden polemic.

Devi's story 'Breast-Giver' is translated by Spivak as part of her discussion of the work of the Subaltern Studies Group. The group's aim is to re-articulate the insurgent role of marginalised tribal groups in the Indian independence movement which has been largely chronicled in terms of bourgeois nationalist activists. This aim demands at least a pragmatic belief in the existence of the silenced subaltern as agent of revolutionary struggle. To produce this 'effect of an operating subject' (*Other Worlds*, 204), the group reads official documents as hidden polemics. Official accounts are perceived as shaped by the dialogic impress of insurgent consciousness, to which the official voice of the documents is, in a sense, responding. That negative inscription or hidden polemic produces, as its reverse, the positive figuring of the subaltern's political consciousness. So too with Devi's prose: the ironising negation, in her stories, of precisely registered social perspectives can only derive from a specific, politically-positioned narrative consciousness. This location in 'once-occurrent' time and space produces the compelling obligation to speak out *this* word on behalf of the perceived needs of the other as conscripted female identity. However, the scepticism which is the generative principle of narrative discourse ensures that 'this' word never postures as the last or final word.

Spivak allows that a strategic fiction of identity constructed in 'a scrupulously visible political interest' might offer a solution to the current problem brought about by poststructuralist emptying of the subject position (*Other Worlds*, 205). I suggest that the various forms of 'sceptical commitment' or ambivalent positioning I have located in women's writing might be brought into productive conjunction with Spivak's sense of strategic fiction. A fiction, even if strategic, does not necessarily prevent an identifying over-investment; only an ambivalent position both inside and outside the discourse can ensure this. Women characters in Carter's last books perform strategically but lovingly in answer to the visible and vital needs of others. They commit themselves to the practice required by a social exigency, yet they always remain sceptical spectators of their own performance.

In the Name of Bakhtin:
Appropriation and Expropriation in Recent Russian and Western Bakhtin Studies

Carol Adlam

> To imitate or to apply Bakhtin, to read him by engaging him in a dialogue, betrays what is most valid in his work.
>
> –Paul de Man

> It seems to me that we must leave Bakhtin in peace. [...] Only then will his name not be scattered in fragments of citations, and will it acquire an actual infinity, unconditional upon a chronotope.
>
> –A.V. Bosenko

> The native [Russian] researcher or even the 'inquisitive Scythian' who becomes acquainted with foreign textual and extra-textual 'discourses' in general and with interpretations of Bakhtin in particular at times feels as though he is in a dream [...]
>
> –Vitalii Makhlin

> [...] and this is what exasperates me above all, or, to express myself even more strongly, arouses disbelief and utter dismay—the fact that one often comes across tendencies in literary and cultural criticism which yield to the preference for the view from within, i.e., for the idea that the most successful and even the sole possible method for the study of the subject consists in being that which is studied.
>
> –Caryl Emerson

The overwhelming quantity of Bakhtin-related material produced over the last few years might well encourage the hapless commentator to start by concluding that Bakhtin's significance in the humanities is self-evident,[1] and, other than adding that Bakhtin's name has now travelled beyond even the walls of academe into various forms of popular culture,[2] to retire with the satisfaction of a job well done. Tempting

---

[1] At the most recent count, for instance, the number of entries in the Bakhtin Centre's on-line database had reached over 1500; see URL: http://www.shef.ac.uk/academic/A-C/bakh/bakhtin.html. The MLA database also contains at least another 1000 references, not necessarily overlapping. See also Subhash Jaireth, 'Russian and Non-Russian Readings of Bakhtin: Contours of an Emerging Dialogue', *Southern Review*, 28 (March 1995), 20–40; and Craig Brandist, 'British Bakhtinology: An Overview', *Dialog. Karnaval. Khronotop*, 1 (1995), 161–71.

[2] For example: a character in the 1995 film *Smoke* (dir. Wayne Wang; wr. Paul Auster) tells the story of one Mikhail Bakhtin, great Russian philosopher and hardened nicotine-addict, who used the pages of one of his manuscripts as cigarette papers; while *The Guardian* has cited *Rabelais*

though such a course of action may be, it would risk transforming the
expansive heterogeneity of what has come to be known as 'Bakhtin
studies' into an illusory homogeneity, and would ignore the consequences of certain pressing questions about processes of transformation in the vagaries of publication, translation, and application. For,
while the first two decades of Bakhtin's influence in the Western humanities were characterised by an enthusiasm for his appropriateness
to various fields of thought, it is only now, in the current period of ex-
ponential growth, that we can detect an increasing self-reflexivity in
Bakhtin studies which indicates an increasing caution about the appropriateness of these same areas to Bakhtin's own thought. In Bakhtin's
terminology, we might say that the early centrifuge of enthusiasm is
now increasingly being countered by centripetal interventions which
openly revolve around efforts to define, yet again, Bakhtin's 'project'
for the humanities. And at a time when the publication of substantial
archive material seems imminent—material which it seems might entail
a complete re-evaluation of Bakhtin's thought—it seems necessary now
more than ever to consider this central problem as it appears in the
English-speaking world and in Bakhtin's own home land. It is no sur-
prise that Bakhtin's progress in Russia and the West has never been
complementary; what is perhaps less expected is the degree to which
those who cross the divide between the two are not, as we shall see,
always strictly complimentary. It is Bakhtin's own thinking which requires that this be seen as more than the internecine disputes that are an
inevitable by-product of varying points of view within any field of research, and rather as of considerable relevance in shaping how Bakhtin
is understood. Critical debate cannot now assume the mantle of puta-
tive objectivity discarded by philosophical texts; neither can we forget
our inevitable participation in the helix of response and addressivity
that Bakhtin has shown applies always and everywhere, in every discursive situation (including that known as 'Bakhtin studies') and which
at each turn reformulates the subject of discussion. In other words,

---

and His World as the 'pretentious' theoretical equivalent of the 'Carry On' films. These some-
what frivolous examples might serve to disprove Vadim Kozhinov's recent argument in his polemical response to Vitalii Makhlin's 'Bakhtin i Zapad (Opyt obzornoi orientatsii)' [Bakhtin and
the West: An Attempted Overview], *Voprosy filosofii*, 1 (1993), 94–114; 3 (1993), 134–50, that
Bakhtin is known in the West only by a select group of academics, in contrast to his fame in
Russia, which Kozhinov claims was widespread even before the publication of the major works
in the early 1970s. See V.V. Kozhinov, 'Bakhtin i ego chitateli. Razmyshleniia i otchasti
vospominaniia' [Bakhtin and His Readers: Reflections and Partial Recollections], *Dialog. Karnaval. Khronotop*, 2–3 (1993), 120–35.

whether we like it or not, in speaking about Bakhtin we inevitably speak in the name of Bakhtin. Hence this paper will restrict itself to dealing with some recent, representative examples of the 'secondary' material; since it is this that in part represents Bakhtin's potential on his behalf. The first section will discuss some of the overt interventions in this debate; the second will move away from polemics to an examination of practice, since it is in fact in the area of explication and application that the issue of appropriation raises its head in ways which have direct effect on how Bakhtin is understood in the future.

One

The four expressions of disquiet which head this paper are chosen for their varying articulations of this problem. The first, Paul de Man's conclusion to his paper 'Dialogue and Dialogism', is, with the hindsight of the thirteen years since its first publication, remarkable in its exposure of a raw nerve that still troubles Bakhtin studies.[3] Although de Man's criticism of 'application' is directed specifically against a simplistic deployment of Bakhtin's terminology within the parameters of conventional literary theory, it nevertheless lays bare the terms around which today's debate is being conducted: i.e., are extensions (applications) of Bakhtin merely the poor relations of Bakhtin's own work, whose imitation should be seen not so much as flattery, but as an attempt to denude his legacy of its riches? Is it the case that in even entertaining the notion of entering into dialogue with Bakhtin we betray one of the central tenets of Bakhtin's thought: that of the non-reiterability of the once-occurrent act and word? De Man's words of warning also testify to a curious shift in the critical discourse of Bakhtin studies, for while the references to 'imitating' or 'applying' Bakhtin, and to 'engaging Bakhtin in a dialogue', might be familiar as *separate* terms to anyone with even a nodding acquaintance with the secondary material, their deployment here as *synonyms* is more likely to be unfamiliar. And it would seem that the very range of the research undertaken 'in the name of Bakhtin' indicates that the distinction between 'valid' and 'imitative' has, simply, fallen apart. Consequently, the idea that this entails some sort of treachery to Bakhtin loses its relevance.

But that would be just too simple. If this issue were indeed resolved, then there would be no uneasy sense of it lying half-buried in the

---

[3] Paul de Man, 'Dialogue and Dialogism', *Poetics Today*, 4. 1 (1983), 98–107 (p. 107).

opening or concluding paragraphs of much Bakhtinian research, and still less would there be the sort of extreme forms of justification, or indeed, refutation, of Bakhtin's standing that is expressed in the work of present-day commentators such as A.V. Bosenko.[4] Bosenko's re-articulation of the specific issue of Bakhtin's 'non-reiterability' is atypical (at least in the forum of Bakhtin studies), yet his conclusion that perhaps the best Bakhtin is one who is, to put it bluntly, dead and buried, might well be seen as the logical extreme of the same issue raised by de Man. Bosenko's objections are brief, and unsupported by other than what, in the context of decades of Soviet hagiography and (anti)historicism, can only be described as highly emotive images of a 'canonised' Bakhtin 'turned into a bronze monument with an out-stretched hand' (Bosenko, 81), a Bakhtin who is at times simply 'vulgar' (*poshl*) in his 'Faustian attempts to reconstruct time', and whose work is a 'theogony which has nothing in common with the commodity circulation of the contemporary sciences' (Bosenko, 84). However, this iconoclastic objection to Bakhtin's ubiquity represents not just an attempt to protect Bakhtin from the market forces governing the contemporary humanities, but equally a bid to protect contemporary humanities from the insidious influence of Bakhtin. Bosenko's view of both Bakhtin and the contemporary humanities is expressed as follows:

> Evidently, one of the reasons for Bakhtin's growing popularity is the decline in general philosophical culture, and the seeming acces-sibility of the meanings of his works [...] His works offer the happy delusion that anyone can, without effort, and with every right, par-ticipate in creation [...] Therein lies the reason for the fact that Bakhtin has no followers, only epigons and imitators. (Bosenko, 85).

Clearly, this evocation of 'epigons and imitators' is resonant of de Man's warning in word only, insofar as Bosenko's dismissal of Bakh-tin as a thinker consigns him to an oblivion which Bosenko himself de-scribes as 'that collapse of inverted time where nothing happens' (Bosenko, 85). While we might justifiably shrug this aside as little more than a *reductio ad absurdum* of the issue of whether we can in-

---

[4] A.V. Bosenko, 'Vlast' vremeni, ili ostav'te Bakhtina v pokoe [The Power of Time, or Leave Bakhtin in Peace], in *M.M. Bakhtin i perspektivy gumanitarnykh nauk: Materialy nauchnoi konferentsii (Moskva, RGGU, 1-3 fevralia 1993 goda)* (So-bytie v nauke; Vitebsk, 1994), pp. 83–5 (p. 85).

deed 'engage Bakhtin in dialogue', Bosenko's reference to 'the decline in general philosophical culture' is significant for its negative signalling of the concerted reassessment of Bakhtin's contemporary philosophical influences which is taking place in Russia.

Vitalii Makhlin is a key figure in this development in Russian Bakhtin studies. In 'Beyond the Text', from which the epigraph is taken,[5] Makhlin begins by raising one of the most vexatious issues of Bakhtin and appropriation: knowledge of the language of the original text. Despite the fact that for Bakhtin all acts of understanding might be seen as acts of 'translation', Makhlin implies that a hierarchy of sorts must be acknowledged in coming to terms with Bakhtin's legacy in its inescapably messy manifestations, reminding us that 'the fact that the majority of those who write and pass judgement about "dialogism" are not Russianists is specifically due to the service of Russianists' ('Beyond the Text', 35). But in calling in the debt to those Russianists who have made access to Bakhtin's work possible, Makhlin intends more than to labour the obvious point that the fidelity of translated material which comes to non-Russianists lies inevitably beyond their control.[6] In fact, Makhlin moves beyond the linguistic issue by offering an account of what he sees as superficially radical theoretical movements of the West, which

> in the Soviet and post-Soviet consciousness are associated with the most crude and aggressive tendencies of Soviet culture, and which have in recent decades [...] enjoyed a sort of 'second wind' in the relatively comfortable and decorous atmosphere of Western aca-

---

[5] Vitalii Makhlin, 'Za tekstom: koe-chto o zapadnoi bakhtinistike s postoiannym obrashcheniem k postsovetskoi. (vmesto obzora)' [Beyond the Text: A Few Words on Western Bakhtin Studies, with Constant Reference to Post-Soviet Bakhtin Studies: In Place of a Survey], in T.G. Iurchenko (ed.), *Bakhtin v zerkale kritiki* (Moscow: Labirint, 1995), pp. 32–55 (p. 39).

[6] The issue of translation and appropriation is directly addressed in A.E. Makhov, 'Perevod - prisvoenie: "chuzhoe slovo" inkognito' [Translation - Appropriation: 'The Alien Word' Incognito], in *M.M. Bakhtin i perspektivy gumanitarnykh nauk*, pp. 109–13, where Makhov argues that the translator's voice has become less discernible over this century. Caryl Emerson (translator of the texts in *The Dialogic Imagination*, and of *Problems of Dostoevsky's Poetics*) also raises the issue in her review essay of Michael Gardiner, *The Dialogics of Critique: M.M. Bakhtin and the Theory of Ideology* (1992), 'Getting Bakhtin, Right and Left', *Comparative Literature*, 46.3 (1993), 288–303. Here Emerson criticises Gardiner (who does not read Russian) for his practice of parenthetically including the original Russian terminology in the text, writing that 'the rule of thumb here is: if you don't know a language it's best not to fake it' (p. 301, note 12). In a polemic with Caryl Emerson and Gary Saul Morson, Antony Wall and Clive Thomson have written that 'There is no one language, natural or artificial, that guarantees access to the truth; certainly knowledge of the Russian language that Bakhtin spoke and wrote does not', 'Cleaning Up Bakhtin's Carnival Act', *Diacritics*, 23.2 (Summer 1993), 47–70 (p. 49).

demic 'theory', which has deconstructed latter-day theoretical constructs whilst preserving and even strengthening latter-day
'theoretism' ('Beyond the Text', 42–3).

For Makhlin, both this Western 'distortion' and its post-Soviet, naively
spiritualist 'Double' fail to understand Bakhtin's true contribution to
the humanities: the production of a new consciousness based upon the
dialogic subject. This will be understood by Western scholars in the
humanities only when

> the 'canonical' nature of specialization ceases to be associated
> with—I will express myself sharply—the logocentric triflings of
> 'materialism', 'the unconscious', 'feminism', 'class', and other at-
> tempts to distinguish oneself from one's own generality or to give
> oneself value in the eyes of this generality whilst 'effacing' and de-
> nying it. For post-Soviets, when it ceases to be associated with [...]
> 'spirituality', 'principle', monologic all-embracing 'unity' [*vse-
> edinstvo*], intuited and structured in the spirit of Western 'struc-
> turalism' and 'semiotic totalitarianism' ('Beyond the Text', 47).

Makhlin's misgivings about the capabilities of Western and post-Soviet
interpreters to succeed in the task of reconstituting Bakhtin's true place
in the humanities are founded on a fundamental given of reception
grounded far 'beyond the text'. The problematics of the Western context in particular, the unfamiliar terrain in which the bewildered 'in-
quisitive Scythian'[7] wanders, are more clearly explained in Makhlin's
contemporaneous piece, 'The Third Renaissance'.[8] Here, Makhlin
painstakingly reconstructs an 'unofficial' line of philosophical-aesthetic
thought of the 1920s in Russia, thereby challenging the belief that one
of the deleterious consequences of the rise of the avant-garde movement and the subsequent imposition of Socialist Realist doctrine was
the emergence of a philosophical vacuum. This vast recuperative un-
dertaking is dually motivated:[9] firstly, by the challenge to evade ways

---

[7] The Scythians were among the first invaders of the early Slav settlements (now in the Ukraine).
The term usually carries a pejorative connotation (cf. 'Barbarians' in English), but here Makhlin
uses it to emphasise that even the most idly curious of Russian readers who happened upon a
Western interpretation of Bakhtin would be struck by its strangeness.
[8] V.L. Makhlin, 'Tretii Renessans' [The Third Renaissance], in K.G. Isupov (ed.), *Bakhtin-
ologiia: Issledovaniia, perevody, publikatsii (k stoletiiu rozhdeniia Mikhaila Mikhailovicha
Bakhtina)* (St. Petersburg: Aleteiia, 1995), pp. 132–54.
[9] See, for instance, V. L. Makhlin, 'Dialog kak sposob novogo myshleniia: (kul'turologicheskaia
kontseptsiia M.M. Bakhtina i sovremennost')' [Dialogue as a Means for New Thinking: Mikhail
Bakhtin's Culturological Concept and Contemporaneity], in *Chelovek v zerkale kul'tury i obra-
zovaniia* (Moscow, 1988), pp. 82–91; 'Bakhtin i "karnavalizatsiia soznaniia" gumanitarnykh

of thinking that manifest theoretism in any way; and secondly by the need, as Makhlin sees it, to face the fact that this must begin with a re-assessment of contemporary ways of thought, particularly those which claim to be radically subversive. The 'unofficial' layer of thought which lies beyond either the most obvious 'official' and the avant-garde 'anti-official' has been usurped by the monologisms of modern-ism and subsequently, by its own 'inversion' of post-modernism ('The Third Renaissance', 150). For Makhlin, these two domains (and their discourses of autonomous individualism and anti-individualism) are perfidious not just because they obscure the 'unofficial' tradition of thought with a love of abstraction that is conducive to theoretism, but more importantly, because their flagship iconoclasm is in fact con-doned by, and essential to, 'official' culture. Therefore to attempt to appropriate Bakhtin into any of the discourses that have emerged from the movements of the avant-garde in the West, as well as in Russia (structuralism, poststructuralism, etc.) is an error. Makhlin's excoriat-ing remarks about Western Bakhtinians arise at least in part from his insistent objection that an (at least) three-stage sequence of usurpations by pretender discourses ('logocentric triflings') has occurred, each in-verting the other to produce increasingly distorted (what he describes elsewhere as 'grotesque-anachronistic')[10] reversals of its predecessor. It is a nonsense to hope that this chain of 'inversion of inversions' will ever somehow arrive at the 'true' Bakhtin, since, quite simply, every new manifestation of these 'other, dialogizing backgrounds' are all launched along the same misdirected trajectory.

This distinction is important. Tracing a path 'back' along this trajec-tory, we see that Makhlin does not present us with a crude conception of what a 'true' Bakhtin might look like, but instead suggests Bakhtin's participation in a largely unexplored community of thinkers.[11] Indeed, the 'true' Bakhtin is for Makhlin far more a chronotope of shared, yet differently developed ideas than a single individual with a canon of be-

---

nauk' [Bakhtin and the 'Carnivalization of Consciousness' in the Human Sciences], in *M.M. Bakhtin i perspektivy gumanitarnykh nauk*, pp. 7–16.

[10] Makhlin, 'Bakhtin i "karnavalizatsiia soznaniia" gumanitarnykh nauk', p. 7. It is certainly the case that Makhlin's descriptions elsewhere of other Bakhtin practitioners are far from temperate, but as I have tried to demonstrate in this extended explication, they are founded in an argument that deserves attention.

[11] Makhlin began this argument in his contribution to a conference held in Orel in 1993, pub-lished as 'Russkii neklassicheskii gumanitet 20–kh godov XX veka (neopoznannaia para)' [The Russian non-Classical Humanities of the 1920s: an Unacknowledged Pair], in *Bakhtinskie chteniia. Filosofskie i metodologicheskie problemy gumanitarnogo poznaniia* (OGTRK: Orel, 1994), pp. 37–45.

liefs to be implemented. The contrast between his approach and that
expressed by Sergei Bocharov (the surviving executor of Bakhtin's
estate) in his biographical piece 'The Event of Being' is instructive.[12]
In his discussion of the events of Bakhtin's life, Bocharov laments the
'Bakhtinian mass-cult', and 'this vulgar Bakhtinism which has flour-
ished around his name', but comforts himself with the idea that 'the
core of his [Bakhtin's] thought remains untouchable and fairly secret'
(Bocharov, 219). While Makhlin's and Bocharov's views might coin-
cide superficially (Bocharov might welcome, for example, Makhlin's
call for a 'moratorium' on appropriation), they are fundamentally at
odds insofar as Makhlin cannot be accused of a form of nostalgia for a
lost paradise of thought or thinker.[13] Rather, Makhlin's call for this
reconsideration of Bakhtin would be impossible without in fact being in
our own particular location in the *here and now*:

> One must live in a time like the present, in an epoch, on the one
> hand, of the 'deconstruction' of the whole world and of any right to
> myth, and on the other hand, of a peculiar 'compensation' for that
> tendency, which is expressed in the utterly artificial ideological
> simulacra of mythology (a deconstruction 'exactly on the con-
> trary'). ('The Third Renaissance', 143)

Just as Makhlin describes Aleksandr Ukhtomskii's realisation of the
impossibility of the experimenter being outside the experiment ('The
Third Renaissance', 137) so too the very fact of our distance from
Bakhtin makes a pure, neutral 'return', a removal of our own ideological baggage and an assumption of this thought impossible. What is
possible, Makhlin argues, is a reconstruction of the conditions of this
thought, but here a logical paradox in terms of Makhlin's own thought
arises, in that what at times seems like impatience with the discourses
of the present can, from this perspective, appear as no less than a call

---

[12] S.G. Bocharov, ' Sobytie bytiia' [The Event of Being], *Chelovek*, 4 (1993), 137–8. Full version
published as 'Sobytie bytiia: o Mikhaile Mikhailoviche Bakhtine', *Novyi mir*, 11 (1995), 211–21.
[13] However, Bocharov's wish to limit Bakhtinian research to the study of the primary texts alone
is in sharp contrast to Makhlin's argument in 'Beyond the Text'. Even more striking is Bocharov's view that not only has this 'mass-cult' been a failure in methodological terms (he re-
peatedly stresses that Bakhtin's thought was never suited to be turned into a 'movement' or
'school'), but also that this failure is common knowledge. He writes that '[...] and at some point
it was discovered that Bakhtin's terms do not work (or work badly) beyond the limits of his texts,
and are no good for general academic usage [*ne godiatsia dlia obshchenauchnogo
upotrebleniia*]', 'The Event of Being', p. 219.

for those same discourses to acknowledge their ineluctable part in this radical reconsideration of Bakhtin.[14]

But before we can approach this state, we must return to the problem of what it means to 'engage in a dialogue with Bakhtin'. Makhlin illustrates this by ending with a discussion of Bakhtin's much-cited statement that 'Nothing is absolutely dead: every meaning will have its homecoming festival' ('The Third Renaissance', 150). His choice of this quotation, so lyrically reassuring in its promise of a prodigal's welcome to every semantic resurrection, bears directly on the question of appropriation. Indeed, Makhlin need do no more than ask the question that this quote begs in order to make his point: 'What does this mean? That is, what does this mean *for us*?' ('The Third Renaissance', 150), although he hammers it home with a typically acerbic dismissal of the notion that being well-versed in esoteric terminology is somehow *Bakhtin's* point:

> Today, liberal deconstructionists, politicians, fools, former party workers and former ardent Marxists, pretenders of all colours, all gabble this discourse [*etot diskurs dobaltyvaiut*] ('The Third Renaissance', 151).

Makhlin's article is significant if for no other reason than that he dares to ask the question, 'what does this mean *for us*?'

Makhlin's rhetoric is almost uncannily echoed by Caryl Emerson, who, like him, locates herself in a mediatory position between the West and Russia. Like Makhlin, Emerson criticises the ubiquitous urge to politicise Bakhtin, commenting on Western Bakhtinians' 'extraordinary and unhealthy interest in questions of the body',[15] and referring elsewhere to 'the currently fashionable liberationist triad: race, class, gen-

---

[14] This hermeneutic argument contrasts with Anthony Wall's and Clive Thomson's view in 'Cleaning Up Bakhtin's Carnival Act' (see note 6), where they argue that 'we shall never know his personal views on particular questions of his time. It is equally obvious that we shall never know what his views *would have been* on issues of our time [...] We would claim that no such mystical *unio* is possible, at least on this earth', p. 48.

[15] 'Stoletnii Bakhtin v angloiazychnom mire glazami perevodchika' [The Centegenarian Bakhtin in the Anglophone World through the Eyes of a Translator], *Voprosy literatury* (May-June 1996), 68–81. In her discussion, Emerson differentiates the Western approach and Russian approaches to the question of the body, and argues that Russian researchers view Bakhtin's notion of the body 'more soberly' than their Western counterparts, who reduce Bakhtin's concept to 'a theory of the grotesque and the erotic' (p. 78). Emerson concludes that 'the goal of Bakhtin's investigations was utterly defined: body and flesh, from his point of view, are fundamentally intended for the concrete dispersal of us in space as unique, unsubstitutable individualities, and *not* in order to include us in some sort of grouping of "collectives"' (p. 78).

der'.[16] But here the issue of appropriation emerges specifically as *ex-propriation*, since for Emerson, Bakhtin is not just 'distorted', but is potentially dispossessed of the territory she charts on his behalf: indeed it might appear that it is only Emerson's indefatigable willingness to put her finger in the dyke that saves Bakhtin from being swept away in a tidal wave of 'isms'. In defending Bakhtin's ground, Emerson is obliged to employ an elaborate rhetorical gesture in order to place herself (and her anticipated interlocutor, the Russian Bakhtinian) firmly within the bastion walls, as the follow-on from the epigraph illustrates:

> [T]hus, the right to specialization in subjects linked with questions of feminism belongs exclusively to women; Negroes alone are accepted in the Afro-American section; people of Eastern descent in the East-Asian section, while they attempt to turn away [*otvadit'*] those who do not belong to any given group because they do not consider them to be sufficiently competent.[17]

This depiction of an anarchic hyper-territorialism in the Western humanities really works in reverse: rather than mapping out the other's territory, it functions to chart out Emerson's, and by extension, Bakhtin's.[18] Thus, Bakhtin's solidly conservative, 'apolitical' credentials are reclaimed, and in the Russian context he becomes, as Emerson asserts, 'a rather conservative thinker', a 'philosopher of life', and 'no apostle of carnival and certainly not of trend-setting literary theory' (*Fruits of Her Plume*, 14).

Two

This distinction between two views of Bakhtin (here delineating a convenient Russia/West disjuncture) is best illustrated through an examination of some recent applications.[19] For all that it is understood that

---

[16] Caryl Emerson, 'Bakhtin and Women: A Nontopic with Immense Implications', in Helena Goscilo (ed.), *Fruits of Her Plume: Essays on Contemporary Russian Women's Culture* (London; New York: M.E. Sharpe, 1993), pp. 3–20 (p. 3).

[17] Caryl Emerson, 'Bakhtin, periferiia i vnenakhodimost': o tsennosti otchuzhdeniia ot samogo sebia i ot rodnogo doma' [Bakhtin, the Periphery, and Outsideness: On the Value of Alienation from Oneself and One's Native Home], *Diapazon*, 1 (1993), 51–8 (p. 52).

[18] See also Caryl Emerson, 'The Shape of Russian Cultural Criticism in the Postcommunist Period', *Canadian Slavonic Papers*, 34.4 (1992), in which Emerson defines 'feminism' according to her own terms ('a gender-sensitive reading of, say, Shakespeare or Rabelais'), and then dismisses it on the grounds of that same definition: 'the above-mentioned gynocentric reading of Shakespeare would be, I'm afraid, "racism by gender"' (p. 368).

[19] In contrast, Michael Holquist has commented that 'the fact that Bakhtin continues to worry so unfashionable a problem as the relation of life to literature, is, it seems to me, a good thing', in

this disjuncture emerges from the discrepancy of subject matter, although not discourse, between Bakhtin's earlier and later works, as
well as the circumstances of their initial reception, the debate over how
to define Bakhtin is none the less heated.[20] It seems that this continuing dispute over Bakhtin's status has been heightened by the recent
publication of a substantial quantity of archival material in Russia,[21]
and Bakhtin's credentials as a purely 'literary' thinker' have been
specifically problematised by the publication of transcripts of lengthy
taped interviews with Bakhtin made by Viktor Duvakin in the early
1970s.[22] Despite this, it is significant that four of the keynote addresses at the Centenary Conference in Moscow in 1995 have recently
been published in the Russian journal *Voprosy literatury* [Questions of
Literature] under the rubric of 'Bakhtin and Contemporary Literary
Scholarship',[23] which perhaps heralds the re-emergence of this topic as

---

'Dialogue: Conversation between Robert F. Barsky and Professor Michael Holquist.*Hamden
CT, Saturday-Sunday August 18–19, 1990', in Michael Holquist and Robert F. Barsky (eds.),
Social Discourse/Discours social, 3.1/2 (Spring-Summer 1990), 1–22 (p. 17).

[20] See V.V. Zdol'nikov, 'Sporiat bakhtinovedy (zametki o nauchnoi konferentsii v MGU im.
M.V. Lomonosova)' [Arguments between Bakhtin Scholars: Notes on a Conference at the M.V.
Lomonosov Moscow State University'], *Dialog. Karnaval. Khronotop*, 1 (1992), 138–41;
'Vopros ostaetsia otkrytym (nemnogo sub"ektivnye zametki o konferentsii "Bakhtin i perspektivy
gumanitarnykh nauk", Moskva, RGGU, fevral' 1993 goda)' [The Question Remains Open: A
Few Subjective Notes on the Conference 'Bakhtin and Prospects for the Humanities', Moscow,
RGGU, February 1993], *Dialog. Karnaval. Khronotop*, 2–3, 1993), 198–201; 'Drugoi Bakh-
tin?..Ili drugie - my?' [Is Bakhtin Other? Or are We?], *Dialog. Karnaval. Khronotop*, 2 (1995),
182–90.

[21] The Russian journal *Dialog. Karnaval. Khronotop* has since published material ranging from
correspondence between Bakhtin and V.N. Turbin, M.I. Kagan (1, 1992), and L.E. Pinskii (2,
1994); testimonies by Bakhtin's acquaintances such as R.M. Mirkina (1, 1993), M.V. Iudina (4,
1993); A. Vulis (2-3, 1993); V.V. Kozhinov (2–3, 1993; 2, 1994); D.S. Likhachev (1, 1995);
previously unpublished material by Bakhtin such as notes from lectures on Russian literature (1,
1993; 2, 1995); further notes toward the re-working of the *Dostoevkii* book (1, 1994); and a full
transcript of Bakhtin's defence of his dissertation (2–3, 1993).

[22] V.D Duvakin, 'Pepel i almaz: Iz rasskazov M.M. Bakhtina, zapisannykh V.D. Duvakinym',
[Ash and Diamond: from Conversations with Bakhtin, Recorded by V.D. Duvakin], *Literatur-
naia gazeta*, 4 August 1993, 6; V.D. Duvakin, 'Razgovory s M.M. Bakhtinym' [Conversations
with Bakhtin], *Chelovek*, 4–6 (1993); 1–4 (1994). Indeed, in answer to Duvakin's question of
whether he considers himself more philosopher than philologist, Bakhtin replies unequivocally,
'I am a philosopher. I am a thinker'.

[23] The papers published under the rubric 'Bakhtin i sovremennoe literaturovedenie', *Voprosy
literatury*, (May-June, 1996) were: Caryl Emerson's 'The Centegenarian Bakhtin' (see note 15);
N. Nikolaev, '"Dostoevskii i antichnost'" kak tema Pumpianskogo i Bakhtina (1922–1963)'
[Dostoevskii and Antiquity' as a Theme in Pumpianskii and Bakhtin], 115–27; V.L. Makhlin,
'Litsom k litsu: programma M.M. Bakhtina v arkhitektonike bytiia-sobytiia XX veka', 82–8
['Face to Face: Bakhtin's Programme in the Architectonics of Being as Event in the Twentieth
Century', in *Face to Face: Bakhtin in Russia and the West* (Sheffield: Sheffield University Press,
1997)]; Igor Shaitanov, 'Zhanrovoe slovo u Bakhtina i formalistov', 89–114 ['The Generic Word
in Bakhtin and the Formalists', in *Face to Face*]. The pieces are prefaced by an introduction by
Vitalii Makhlin (65–7).

a salient feature of Russian Bakhtin studies in the future.[24]   Whether
entirely successful or not in the overt intention to revive this topic, the
approaches of the four pieces indicate a significant variation in approaches to the question of literary studies and Bakhtin in the West and
in Russia.[25] Igor Shaitanov's and Nikolai Nikolaev's papers deal directly with Bakhtin's contemporaneous contexts, indicating a tendency
to expound rather than 'apply' Bakhtin in Russia, even in the subject of
Russian literary studies. In the West, by contrast, Bakhtin's view of
literature is seen far more as an extended, or 'meta'-metaphor of life. A
rather untypical Russian illustration of this view is provided by the
Russian cultural historian Vladimir Bibler, who suggests that literature
for Bakhtin functions as a means to reformulate philosophical concerns
without being trapped in traditional philosophical categories: for him,
Bakhtin was primarily a philosopher who studied philosophy, as he
puts it, 'through the eye of the needle of literature'.[26] The literary text
is also relegated, albeit to different ends, to the peripheries of research
in some of the assertions made by the American scholar Michael Bernard-Donals, particularly in '"Discourse in Life": Answerability in
Language and the Novel', where he bluntly states that 'Bakhtin is not
concerned with literary theory per se', but rather he 'outlines a "social"
theory [...] "illustrated by" literary models'.[27] In his recent monograph
Bernard-Donals proceeds to problematise this idea of direct, model-
like correlation between text and context, by analysing in detail the
tension arising from Bakhtin's seemingly contradictory presentations of
dialogic relations in life as a given, and dialogic manifestations of
written discourse as historically, and 'ideologically' produced out of
complex socio-political historical factors.[28] In ultimately favouring the
implications of Bakhtin's demonstration of the ideological production
(and permeation) of discourse, Bernard-Donals reinscribes literature
and literary criticism's place in the 'totality of human culture' as no

---

[24] It will be interesting to observe the disparity between this and the next international conference which is to take place in June 1997 in Calgary. Publicity material indicates that the bias of
the conference might be away from strictly 'literary' concerns and lean rather more toward the
'sociological'.
[25] This is to discount Emerson's contribution, which is a personalised history of her changing
encounter with Bakhtin through her extensive translation of his work.
[26] Daniel Aleksandrov and Anton Struchkov, 'Bakhtin's Legacy and the History of Science and
Culture: An Interview with Anatolii Akhutin and Vladimir Bibler', *Configurations*, 1.3 (1993)
(unpag.), URL:http://muse.jhu.edu/journals/configurations/v001/1.3alexandrov+struchkov.html
[27] Michael Bernard-Donals, '"Discourse in Life": Answerability in Language and the Novel',
Studies in the Literary Imagination, 23.1 (1990), 45–63.
[28] Michael Bernard-Donals, *Mikhail Bakhtin: Between Phenomenology and Marxism*
(Cambridge: CUP, 1995).

longer merely reflective or disinterested, but in fact vitally engaged in the task of understanding and transforming the material conditions of existence.

A slightly different approach is that based upon the implications of Bakhtin's view that 'literature is an inseparable part of the totality of culture and cannot be studied outside the total cultural context' (N70, 139). This perhaps is what has made Bakhtin's investigations particularly amenable to extension and application in other fields of semiotic study,[29] which might perhaps fall within the purview of what Clive Thomson has described as 'dialogic criticism', i.e., that which examines the larger historical and cultural context, as well as internal polyphonic heterogeneity.[30] Indeed, the source of this internal heterogeneity has been shifted away from the text itself, away from the author, to the problematics of reception. In the long feminist tradition of reading 'against the grain' this allows the editors of the 1994 collection *A Dialogue of Voices: Feminist Literary Theory and Bakhtin* to write that feminist dialogics suggests a politics of revealing the voices of the oppressed (Hohne and Wussow, pp. vii-xiii). In a monograph on Gothic fiction, Jacqueline Howard also undertakes a feminist reading of a genre by emphasising that the contextual and institutional nature of interpretation is what determines a text's 'novelness' or otherwise: 'it is always the specific conjectural status of particular discourses, rather than any inherent qualities, which gives those discourses a particular political force'.[31] Similarly, a re-reading both of the political contexts of Bakhtin's works and other works of the Soviet period is carried out by M. Keith Booker and Dubravka Juraga, in their 1995 study *Bakhtin, Stalin, and Modern Russian Fiction*.[32] The work undertaken here is further extended in a 1995 collection edited by Clive Thomson and Hans Raj Dua, entitled *Dialogism and Cultural Criticism*, in which

---

[29] See, for instance, Robert Stam, *Subversive Pleasures: Bakhtin, Cultural Criticism, and Film* (Baltimore; London : Johns Hopkins University Press, 1989); Robert Cunliffe, 'Charmed Snakes and Little Oedipuses: The Architectonics of Carnival and Drama in Bakhtin, Artaud, and Brecht', in *Critical Studies*, 3.2–4.1/2, *Bakhtin and Other Subjects* (1993), 48–69; virginia l. purvis-smith, 'ideological becoming: mikhail bakhtin, feminine écriture, and julia kristeva' [sic], in Karen Hohne and Helen Wussow (eds.), *A Dialogue of Voices: Feminist Literary Theory and Bakhtin* (London, Minneapolis: University of Minnesota Press, 1994), pp. 42–58.

[30] Thierry Belleguic and Clive Thomson, 'Dialogic Criticism', in *Encyclopedia of Contemporary Literary Theory: Approaches, Scholars, Terms* (Buffalo; Toronto; London: University of Toronto Press, 1993), pp. 31–4.

[31] Jacqueline Howard, *Reading Gothic Fiction: A Bakhtinian Approach* (Oxford: Clarendon Press, 1994), p. 51.

[32] M. Keith Booker and Dubravka Juraga, *Bakhtin, Stalin, and Modern Russian Fiction: Carnival, Dialogism, and History* (London; Westport, Connecticut: Greenwood Press, 1995).

several of the contributors challenge, on the basis of the real experience of post-colonial India, interpretations of dialogism which make
unproblematised assumptions about literary texts and social or political
linguistic practice.[33]

The proceedings of the 1994 conference *Bakhtin and Prospects for
the Human Sciences* approach literary studies rather differently, by at-
tempting to historicise Bakhtin,[34] and by providing some detailed
evaluations of the methodology of the study of literature and of the
components of the internal stratification of written discourse. N.D.
Tamarchenko, for example, insists on the importance of attending to
the problem of the 'inner dialogism' of the artistic word, and concludes
that the significance of the novel genre lies in its ability to activate the
latent dialogism of spoken discourse.[35] Several other articles in this
collection also implicitly follow Bakhtin's prioritising of the novel by
examining the manifestations of the written dialogic word. For instance, L. Chernets suggests a concretisation of Bakhtin's terminology,
proposing that three different sorts of dialogism be distinguished in any
analysis of the literary text's aetiology, function, and structure respectively.[36] Chernets suggests that in his theory of genre and style Bakhtin
proposes an intertextual dialogic relation; in the concept of addressivity
and the alien word Bakhtin anticipates the reader's response in dialogic
understanding between text and context; and that, in the analysis of the
interaction between author and hero undertaken in the studies of Dostoevskii and the essay 'Author and Hero', Bakhtin discusses specifically intratextual dialogic relations. Chernets's argument is supported

---

[33] Clive Thomson and Hans Raj Dua (eds.), *Dialogism and Cultural Criticism*, (London, Canada: Mestengo Press, University of Western Ontario, 1995).
[34] Three papers in particular attempt to place Bakhtin's 'totalizing' tendencies with regard to the text and life within a Russian intellectual context (all are published in *M.M. Bakhtin i Perspektivy gumanitarnykh nauk* (see note 4): N. Bonetskaia, in 'Dialogicheskaia filosofiia M. Bakhtina i ontologicheskoe uchenie o cheloveke' [Bakhtin's Dialogical Philosophy and the Ontological Study of Humankind], pp. 22–5, argues that a philosophical idea of lost unity underpins Bakhtin's work on novelistic discourse; M. Bent, in 'M.M. Bakhtin i "integral'nye" tendentsii v obshchestvennoi i esteticheskoi mysli 20–30-kh godov' [Mikhail Bakhtin and the 'Integral' Tendencies of Social and Aesthetic Thought of the 1920s–1930s], pp. 128–9, similarly attempts to define Bakhtin's work in the context of a quest to establish a 'harmonics of discourse'; and Brian Poole offers an extended discussion of Bakhtin in the history of genre in the context of the German Marburg school of philosophy, in 'Mikhail Bakhtin i teoriia romana vospitaniia' [Mikhail Bakhtin and the Theory of the *Bildungsroman*], pp. 62–72.
[35] N.D. Tamarchenko, '"Vnutrenniaia dialogichnost' " slova i tipologiia romana v rabotakh M.M. Bakhtina' [The 'Inner Dialogism' of the Word and a Typology of the Novel in Mikhail Bakhtin], in *Perspektivy*, pp. 102–109.
[36] L.V. Chernets, 'Printsip "dialogizma" v primenenii k genezisu, funktsionirovaniiu i strukture khudozhestvennogo proizvedeniia' [The 'Dialogical' Principle in its Application to the Genesis, Function and Structure of the Artistic Work], in *Perspektivy*, pp. 101–102.

by I.V. Egorov's consideration of 'The Problem of the Author in Mikhail Bakhtin', which similarly seeks to resolve the long-standing debate about continuity in the literary writings by arguing that both 'Author and Hero' and *Problems of Dostoevsky's Poetics* stand in dialogic relation to each other in that the latter represents an extension of the concerns of the earlier text, by testing concepts of personal interaction in a broader cultural arena.[37]

This intratextual assessment has been accompanied by a necessary discussion of the role of the critic and reader in dialogic understanding, in accordance with Bakhtin's argument that the process of freeing the text from the shackles of monologic explanation begins with criticism's realisation of its own limitations. Dmitrii Bak has considered this problem in his 1990 article 'On the Problem of the Outsideness of the Literary Scholar in Bakhtin's Literary Aesthetics', in which he draws a parallel between the category of the 'act' and the activity of the literary critic in relation to the text. In a further article, entitled 'The Non-Formal Method in Literary Scholarship: On the Problem of the Outsideness of the Literary Scholar', Bak considers author-hero relations in contemporary literature as well as the role of the critic in the light of Bakhtin's injunction that 'in order to understand, it is immensely important for the person who understands to be located outside the object of his or her creative understanding—in time, in space, in culture'.[38] Hence, Bakhtin's work has not only prompted a reassessment of the genres he himself discussed (for example, in the collection already mentioned, S.N. Broitman argues against Bakhtin's condemnation of the lyric), but also of those literary genres which in his own terms would appear to be 'monologic'.

---

[37] I.V. Egorov, 'Problema avtora v estetike M.M. Bakhtina (tezisy doklada)' [The Problem of the Author in Mikhail Bakhtin: Theses for a Paper], in *Perspektivy*, pp. 133–4. Finally, K. G. Isupov envisages a breakdown of the discrete categories of literary criticism into a study of discursive practices, as 'the prose of life' is transformed into 'the life of prose'; see K.G. Isupov, 'Ob istorizme prosaiki (vmesto poslesloviia k fragmentu knigi K. Emerson i G.S. Morsona)' [On the Historicism of Prosaics: In Place of an Afterword to a Fragment of Caryl Emerson and Gary Saul Morson's Book], in *Perspektivy*, pp. 25–30.

[38] D.P. Bak, 'K probleme vnenakhodimosti literaturoveda v esteticheskoi kontseptsii M. Bakhtina' [Towards the Problem of the Outsideness of the Literary Scholar in Bakhtin's Literary Aesthetics], in N.A. Gorbanev (ed.), *Khronotop. Mezhvuzovskii nauchno-tematicheskii sbornik* (Dagestanskii ordena Druzhby Narodov gosudarstvennyi universitet im. V.I. Lenina: Makhachkala, 1990), pp. 47–55; 'Neformal'nyi metod v literaturovedenii (k probleme vnenakhodimosti literaturoveda)' [The Non-Formal Method in Literary Scholarship: On the Problem of the Outsideness of the Literary Scholar], in *Bakhtinskii sbornik*, 2 (1991), 243–64.

The continuing variety of approach in discussion and application of Bakhtin, to which these few examples in one area of his work bear witness, obviously demonstrates that the issue of appropriation and expropriation need not hinder development in Bakhtin studies. However, the issue remains pertinent, and with access to the remainder of Bakhtin's work looming on the horizon, it is a safe bet that it will be even more central to the shape of future 'Bakhtinology'. In that sense, the prospects for the future of Bakhtin studies depend on a recognition of the fact that only when the quest for authority ceases to be concealed in the question of authenticity, will the issue of possession and dispossession be resolved.

Strathclyde Modern Language Studies (New Series)

Volumes published

1. Cinema and Ideology (1996), ed. Eamonn Rodgers